Jivah
World Poetry

Ian Harris

Jivah World Poetry

Hardback Edition First Published in Great Britain by aSys Publishing

Paperback Edition First Published in Great Britain by aSys Publishing

Copyright © Ian Harris 2015

All rights reserved.

No part of this document may be reproduced or transmitted in any form or by any means, electronic, mechanical, photocopying, recording, or otherwise, without prior written permission of the Author.

Disclaimer

This is a work of fiction. Names, characters, businesses, places, events and incidents are either the products of the author's imagination or used in a fictitious manner. Any resemblance to actual persons, living or dead, or actual events is purely coincidental.

I would like to thank very much indeed the Chinese company info@tour-beijing.com.

I am very grateful to them for giving me permission to use some of their beautiful pictures which shows China as a place; a culturally rich country that will soon be the world's
number one economy.

Published by aSys Publishing

http://www.asys-publishing.co.uk

ISBN: 978-0993071867

Dedication

Dear Reader,

I dedicate Jivah Poetry to my Mum who passed away on 31st December 2014  she was 87 years old on 23rd December 2014. My Mum stood up to Doctors and Teachers for four years to make sure that I got a fairly good education at a grammar school despite Doctors and Teachers advising her that because of my epilepsy and the drugs I was taking I should be in a special school for disabled people. I finally had to go to the David Lewis Centre for people with epilepsy but I had received four good years education at the Holt Grammar School in Liverpool first.

My name is Ian Harris and this is my wife Janet. I am Jivah. I am now 66 and I started writing poetry when I was put out of work permanently in March 1994. This was due to my disability which is epilepsy. Health and safety would not cover me. I wrote a poem about Princess Diana in September 1997 which I sent to Earl Spencer and I got a lovely reply. But I could not write poetry for 3 years after that the Princess's death it so affected me as it probably did most of the world.

This poem will be in Jivah People's Poetry.

Some great men and two great women have or had epilepsy for instance:

Entertainment: *Danny Glover, Richard Burton, Martin Kemp, Rik Mayall, George Gershwin, Susan Boyle* and of course *Agatha Christie*.

Sportsmen: *Terry Marsh, Duncan Goodhew, Tony Greig*.

Politics Past: *Napoleon Bonaparte, Vladimir Lenin, Julius Caesar, Franklin D Roosevelt* (32nd President US).

All royalties from this work will be split between five registered charities

- *British Heart Foundation registered charity number 225971*
- *Guide Dogs for the Blind, registered charity number 291646,*
- *MacMillan Cancer Support registered charity number 261017,*
- *Diabetes Research Association registered charity number 299047,*
- *Mersey Region Epilepsy Association registered charity number 504366*

Contents

Dedication iii
China's History 1
Hong Kong 2
Beijing 3
Shanghai 4
Across the Pond 5
The Bad Guys 6
Security 7
Greens 8
Peas in a Pod 9
Charismatic Shark 10
Shark's Autobiography 11
Shark the Dinosaur 12
Exploring 13
Work and our Conditions 14
Junior Surveyor 15
Value if any? 16
Progressive Differences 17
Prospects of Administration 18
Loans and Progress 19
More Drills 20
British Solar Pumps 21
Chinese Interest 22
Oil Rig Pipelines 23
Faster Solar Pumps Needed 24
Insurance and Currency 25

Solar Business too	*27*
African Big Game	*28*
African Carnivores	*29*
Accidental Win	*30*
Kingfisher Is	*31*
Kingfisher Community	*32*
Annual Family Holiday	*33*
Value for Money	*34*
Eating Chinese	*35*
My Favourite Dishes	*36*
Ocean World	*37*
I am a Gentle Giant	*38*
Public Transport on Time	*39*
Power-assisted steering	*40*
Hot House	*41*
Humid Atmosphere	*42*
Corgi	*43*
Knowing One's Place	*44*
Seven Liverpools	*45*
Merseyside's Liverpool	*46*
Scandinavian Cruise	*47*
Fjords from the Sky	*48*
Lark	*49*
Larks' Tune and Territory	*50*
Power Sources	*51*
Harnessing Power	*52*
Wanted Dead	*53*
Red Fox on the move	*54*

The Red Foxes' Future	55
A Safe Haven	56
Four Car Family	57
Verve and Drive	58
Koppites	59
Crooked Police, Press and Government	60
American Wilderness	61
Hunters and Their Prey	62
Heavenly Earth	63
Open Accommodation	64
Australian Resources	65
Politics and way of Life	66
Concorde Experience	67
Concorde is Quality	68
Barn Owl Territory	69
Barn Owl Bird of Prey	70
The Wheel	71
Fuels for Power	72
Our Daily H_2O	73
Water is Life	74
The Importance of Water	75
Troutbeck	76
The Trout Community	77
Family and Neighbours	78
Distant Trout Relatives	79
Enemies at Large	80
Troubeck's Vicious	81
Jivah Poetry Books	82

China's History

China is next with all it's culture class and style,
I must go and walk along China's Great Wall,
Built by China's first Emperor and well worthwhile,
It can be seen from outer space and seen by all.
It was made mainly of earth, stones and wood,
And the earth was a kind of compacted mud.

It goes under hills and there are some breaches,
It was built as fortification with turrets and all,
For five thousand five hundred miles it reaches,
But the Chinese see it is maintained well overall.
Much further than I could go on my motor bike,
And I'll be advised on different parts I might like.

Fifty six different ethnic groups in China belong,
And their economy grows so fast America complain,
With seventeen provinces what could go wrong?
When, all Chinese people work hard for financial gain.
One point two four billion of China's population,
Are Han Chinese by far the largest group in their nation.

Hong Kong is a Province on China's south coast,
Enclosed by the Pearl Delta and the South China Sea,
Part of the PRC but influenced by Britain the most,
And until, 2047 will have a high degree of autonomy.
Hong Kong's governance is theirs to dispense,
But China has their Foreign Affairs and Defence.

After ninety nine years of British Colonial rule,
In nineteen ninety seven British rule ceased,
But English is taught from an early age at school,
And our trading relationship has not decreased.
Hong Kong is the place where East meets west,
With oriental traditions and capitalism at it's best.

Hong Kong

Their education system is like that in England,
And is much better than that in mainland China,
They have nine universities that are quite grand,
And their healthcare system is also much finer.
Hong Kong is one of the healthiest places to live,
With high life expectancies if one can remain active.

I would have to go to Hong Kong Island to see,
Hong Kong's government and Aberdeen Bay,
It's international financial centre is a must be,
All are interesting in their own individual way.
Beijing is over twelve hundred miles away,
And Shanghai is seven hundred still taking all day.

London is the biggest financial city on earth,
Second is Hong Kong, Tokyo or New York is third,
Chinese fast trains will speed you right from their birth,
And their outdoor sports arenas are the last word.
The US banking system is not so efficient or cool,
Insufficient staff and charges they hide as a rule.

Hong Kong is the third largest container port after Singapore,
Shenzhen is fourth and Ningbo is the sixth largest port,
After Busan of Korea fifth but China has plenty more,
Guangzho is seventh, Qingdao is eighth for support.
In the top fifty China has eleven and the US five,
Other countries like Britain need to build to survive.

The world's eighth most traded currency is theirs,
The Hong Kong Dollar is traded in all large banks,
But in Britain's big three is where it best fares,
So, on the international stage it very highly ranks.
Hong Kong law is based on English Common Law,
Not, exactly so but it is there at the core.

Beijing

About eight hundred years Before Christ maybe,
A community was built on a 5,000 foot mound,
So at such an altitude one might not see,
That the, air is not polluted just thin on the ground.
The city walls lived to become medieval,
Then the city expanded with much upheaval.

Various Dynasties started during medieval times,
And under different ones their boundaries did change,
Wars were fought and buried there were their crimes,
Until the 15th century there was many an exchange.
It was first known as Beijing in the first century BC,
And the Chinese name has not changed in history.

Now China's capital is Beijing and it suits it just fine,
Peking was the translation that is a Roman name,
But it has been Beijing officially since 1949,
The name means "Northern Peace" just the same.
Over nineteen and a half million people live there,
And unlike Hong it has very little free healthcare.

Then The People's Republic of China took control,
Mao Zedong declared Beijing the capital in 1949,
Walls were crushed in the sixties to expand on the whole,
And Beijing people speak a Mandarin dialect so fine.
Tianjin Xingang is from where Beijing does export,
And is the, world's eleventh biggest container port.

Chinese families can only have one child by law,
So within ten years; or maybe a lot less,
Forty percent of the workers will be fifty or more,
If China does not act there will be little redress.
The Chinese receive little pension from the state,
Something they must fix not dither or wait.

Shanghai

Shanghai is typical of China's booming mainland,
On the Yangtze River Delta by the East China Sea,
And 80% of China's exports it can withstand,
With fashion, culture, media and so, much industry.
Tourists go to see the City God Temple and the Bund,
Pretty places in here that leave people stunned.

Shanghai's name means above the sea,
It is in Eastern China but it has two airports,
Pudong International Airport is particularly busy,
In fact it is the world's third busiest it is thought.
Before Pudong Hongqiao was the very busy star,
But for the Olympic Games people come from afar.

Shanghai Hongqiao was first built in 1907,
It was used by the Japanese as an air force base,
And it was hosting twenty two airlines by 2011,
But now Shanghai Pudong has taken first place.
Britain opened up Shanghai to much foreign trade,
And in 1863 HSBC financial services were made.

Shantou, Jieyang and Chaozhou are in an urban region,
Which, is the fourth most populated one in China,
With very nearly fourteen million people living there,
Where, the poor are very poor and the rich much finer.
Shantou provides a health service of some sort,
It also hosts utilities, telecommunications and transport.

Shanghai is a twin city to Liverpool, Merseyside,
It's population is twenty three million and rising,
Which, makes Shanghai the biggest city worldwide,
And in summation is this really that surprising.
By tonnage Shanghai is the biggest port I guessed,
Much bigger than Rotterdam or Singapore at their best.

Across the Pond

I am now working as a taxi driver in New York,
It is reminiscent of selling insurance in Scotland,
As nothing these people say when they talk,
Is simple enough for me; a mere mortal to understand.
Their English language is an absolute disgrace,
It is like living in a non-English speaking place.

By the Treaty of Paris they have independence too,
But we should have taught them to speak English first,
It would be advantageous for whatever they next do,
But as for conquering languages they have no great thirst.
Their punctuation is poor and their spelling is appalling,
And an open mouth will show the larynx is not stalling.

Taxi driving in New York is an absolute nightmare,
Firstly they drive on the wrong side of the road,
So here I am in a big bustling city which is where,
Nobody knows me or knows their highway code.
It will probably take me a very long while,
Before I can, adjust to live with their crazy lifestyle.

Every fare I get gives me a handsome tip,
So financially my job is a success and a pleasure,
But on the dialect and the short cuts I have no grip,
Although when I do I will take my share of treasure.
I know about roadside cafes, where and when to eat,
And plane timetables because someone will want a seat.

At the Grande Central someone will always want a cab,
JFK Airport is another very popular pick up spot,
Gathering all this knowledge may be really quite drab,
But if you learn it well, financially you can earn a lot.
Large tippers come from seminars and conventions,
From people of learning with very good intentions.

The Bad Guys

Cab drivers say it is hard work to make enough,
They are right, despite what some people say,
In the Jungle we taxi drivers have it cut rough,
Because the cab needs so many fares to pay its way.
For insurance, maintenance, tax, tolls and fuel,
The costs of running it are particularly cruel.

You could be unfortunate enough to be grounded,
This would mean a day's fares you will have lost,
If your cab has been stolen or impounded,
And then getting it back too is an extra cost.
I had parked and just gone to get a big Mac,
But it was nowhere to be seen when I came back.

I stopped at an unsavoury café that has parking too,
I certainly do not want my cab towed away again,
So I eat here where the food is not cheap but it will do,
In fact it is barely edible but I do not complain.
Also while the Cops are eating their lunch here,
The vandals and thieves just seem to disappear.

A really bad day is when you have your cab towed,
It means productive hours lost as well as paying a fine,
A two hundred dollar fine to put it back on the road,
And this system is of a poisonous detrimental design.
If fewer mistakes were made, less hours would be lost,
Public transport would run smoother, at little extra cost.

The worst problem, of course, in a city like New York,
Is the open, violent attitude that is displayed,
And I do not just mean swearing and abusive talk,
I mean when you are threatened with a sharp blade.
Once before I have had a gun pointed at my head,
I could have had a fatal heart attack or been shot dead.

Security

The best possible security scheme,
Is very loyal, obedient, and fearless too,
In fact two breeds of dogs, working as a team,
Will prove their devotion to you is uniquely true.
For your instructions they will always wait,
Standing there with a particularly, eloquent gait.

Of course dogs all differ from breed to breed,
Corgis for their hearing are alert night and day,
And Doberman Pinschers for ferocity and speed,
So that each dog has it's own role to play.
With expensive alarm systems that you may buy,
Often people just stand, listen and wonder why.

Corgis and Dobermans live with mutual respect,
Is it natural or have they all been trained,
As working for man with a colleague is one concept,
That needs to be cultured and well-maintained.
They do not fight much so nobody gets hurt,
And they work very productively in concert.

The Corgis will hear the very faintest sound,
And awaken the Dobermans from their slumber,
Direct them approximately to where the noise was found,
Then some trespasser could be in very much lumber.
Orders do not need to be given in such a case,
It is their duty, and the Dobermans will chase.

The Doberman Pinschers chase and then guard,
Providing the perpetrator will stand quite still,
Because outrunning a Doberman is particularly hard,
And the Dobermans will catch and attack at will.
Doberman Pinschers will give you no more quarter,
So it could end up with the trespasser's slaughter.

Greens

I am bonded closely with my mates in a cell,
We all sit in straight rows like on a London bus,
And if we are healthy then we will grow quite well,
That is only the most resourceful and healthy ones of us.
There is some nutriment that makes us all grow,
But where about it comes from we do not know.

Tightly all of us peas are bound in this cocoon,
Shortly we will fatten and the pod will expand,
So from their stringy bush, the pods are cut soon,
Then for the fruit the pods are opened by hand.
When each of the pods is opened quite flush,
We green peas only need an encouraging push.

Some peas are bruised and others are too hard,
Some are too soft or they may have a black eye,
Such imperfections will always get them barred,
Because poor quality, like this nobody will buy!
Such peas will always be classed as rejected,
And sold to farmers as pig food to, be collected.

Only healthy, prime, juicy peas succeed,
So now I will make quite a good life for myself,
Frozen and packed so I have not really been freed,
Surely I will not stay on a supermarket shelf.
If we are missed, our "sell by" date may expire,
Then it will be time for all of us to retire.

I hear on the grape vine that retirement for us is bad,
That we could be stolen or sent for pig food,
I believe now that my best chances have all been had,
Because the future is grim and I can only brood.
I need to think hard about what I can do,
There must be an opening but vacancies are few.

Peas in a Pod

We hear too that mushy peas are often on sale,
From takeaways, pubs and fish and chip shops,
Pubs often serve them with steak, chips and ale,
Or lager with mashed potatoes and lamb chops.
  Well the working-classes like them anyway,
  With a cheap fatty meal or a horrid, takeaway.

One fine day we were quite viciously tossed,
We were badly shaken up but not now cold,
And it looks like our pension might be lost,
Being in someone's trolley we will soon be sold.
  Perhaps now we will be left completely alone,
  To, freely refresh ourselves and lighten our tone.

To a lady's home we were taken and left to chill,
  Then the bag was cut so that we were set free,
    Into a saucepan that soon began to fill,
  But we wondered what danger can there be.
  It was not the kind of career one wishes for,
In fact I nearly drowned and now I'm feeling sore.

Those of us peas in the pan were left to cook,
  In salty water that burns my sensitive skin,
    So with this heat and the burns I must look,
Very crinkled on the outside and feel soft within.
  After this ordeal we were left to recuperate,
  By leaving, us, all to lie on this china plate.

The lady sat down and came to eat her meal,
Now it was time she was moving in for the kill,
And I could put up no resistance after this ordeal,
I have been put in her mouth and digested at will.
This is the end for me and I wonder what now awaits,
  Will it be something good or just the Pearly ates?

Charismatic Shark

I am Norman the Shark and I eat mostly fish,
I am not a vegetarian so I often vary my meals,
I sometimes I treat myself to a really special dish,
Like a ray, another shark or some tasty seals.
My teeth can give even a whale quite a bite,
Because I am Norman the fierce Great White.

My skin's colour is between black and a salty grey,
I measure about twenty foot from head to fin,
And over to two and a tons is about what I weigh,
So I am the ferocious monster with a fierce wide grin.
My acute sense of smell comes from my nostrils,
And I only breathe through my powerful gills.

If in the water there are a few drops of blood,
I can smell it from up to three miles away,
And whilst my sight and hearing are no good,
Many kinds of animals I will catch and slay.
Many attacks I make I do not mean to kill,
Just sample something or a nip to disturb a dill.

When I migrate we stop at the White Shark Cafe,
It is between Baja and Hawaii in the Pacific Ocean,
It is three thousand feet down, well out of the way,
An ideal place to rest where there is no commotion.
If I stayed at that depth the pressure would surely crush me,
So I regularly surface to escape the force deep in the sea.

Out of every one hundred attacks every year,
Thirty percent are attributed to the Great White,
My mere presence can spread panic and fear,
Whilst I am cruising before I have even taken a bite.
Many animals I bite I do not kill but often maim,
And the severity is exaggerated I have to claim.

Shark's Autobiography

We are solitary animals sometimes seen in pairs,
And the female is always bigger than the male,
Reproduction is really only like having affairs,
Because we just fertilise the eggs inside the female.
There is no placenta so before birth there is a trend,
That always for themselves the pups will have to fend.

When eggs hatch then they need to be nourished,
So unfertilised eggs and smaller siblings they eat,
Until it becomes clear that the fittest have flourished,
And when they are born they are about five feet.
Usually between two and fourteen pups are born,
By eating fish and other sharks their life will dawn.

I usually cruise at about five miles per hour,
But like a Cheetah I can produce bursts of speed,
And for a short while I will have the power,
To, swim at about thirty miles per hour for a feed.
I am forty years old and well into my prime,
And I will live to be sixty given the right time.

I swim predominately where the water is warm,
I go unnoticed in the silent shallow sea pools,
Except for noisy children it is quiet and without alarm,
Until I ferociously strike on these naïve fools.
I dominate fiercely the ocean and the sea,
Where, only stupid humans trespass near me.

Man and the fish that have a stiff backbone,
Have such limited turns and a slow speed as well,
But if I am good-natured I will leave them alone,
As mans' defence is only a cylindrical metal shell.
Sharks silently patrol all of the sea, deaf and blind,
With, there being over three hundred different kind.

Shark the Dinosaur

All Sharks are very fierce and too proud to lose,
If men dare to trespass, it might mean their fate,
I will kill men, but to eat them I do not choose,
Because the taste of a human does not suit my palate!
Few Sharks are brave enough to tackle man,
But with teeth like mine I am one who can.

Man invades my sun drenched white beaches,
Just like a Cuckoo steals another bird's nest,
They invade our waters and stick like leeches,
They damage the coral reef and are quite a pest.
I have an extremely good nose you can tell,
Without sight or hearing I rely solely upon smell.

Just like Eels, we Sharks have no rigid backbone,
So we can turn very quickly to catch our prey,
Our speed and voraciousness is very well-known,
And only a whale might live to die another day.
Some Sharks don't bother with small fish to eat,
And cod, herring and haddock are not such a treat.

I have a cartilaginous body that is torpedo shaped,
I have three thousand teeth and very strong jaws,
A large dorsal fin and two pectoral fins are draped,
And I am descended from the Magalodon dinosaurs.
We, Carcharodon Carcharias are a mighty predator,
Even if we are smaller than relatives, that came before.

In icy cold dirty water about a thousand feet deep,
Tiger Sharks live, breathe and lay in the very dark,
They are nocturnal and in caves for days they can sleep,
The Tiger has stripes but they are still a shark.
In prehistoric times over four hundred million years ago,
The number of forty foot shark-like, creatures began to grow.

Exploring

We worked long hours with much sweat and toil,
Our poor cattle had next to nothing to eat,
And we could not grow much at all in the soil,
Just some corn and sometimes some wheat.
Please look Lord I am down on my knees,
Can we have some luck to help us soon please?

One day we found a big hole in the ground,
So naturally we had to go inside to see,
In the murky darkness we foraged around,
To see what mystery inside there might be.
The walk home afterwards was five miles,
Through dirty rivers then over hills and stiles.

After such a tiresome but an exciting roam,
All our feet were bleeding and aching,
Our hair was dirty and needed a good comb,
And all our backs were bent and breaking.
At home I lit the fire to warm the place,
And I slept deeply with a glow on my face.

We all arose early after a very sound sleep,
Then we had some ears of corn for breakfast,
And thought about that curious hole so deep,
And could it really make us any richer at last.
So we had to travel in hope back to this pass,
Taking, our, picks our shovels and the ass.

Perhaps it has minerals that we could mine,
And we might be lucky and find a rich vein,
We all worked hard but of gems there was no sign,
Despite; gold and silver; being in this terrain.
If we persevered then minerals might bear fruit,
Or would we be poor miners with no prospect of loot.

Work and our Conditions

We all worked, digging extremely hard all day,
Cramped in the dark, all damp and cold,
Because corn farming was not going to pay,
So we fervently looked again for minerals like gold.
Deep down out of the walls, it began to pour,
A thick black liquid we had never seen before.

This is a mystery but it is our most lucrative find,
This is aptly called Black Gold or Texas Tea,
Because it is oil or petrol when it's been refined,
It is ours but we need to make a claim legally.
If there is an oil-lake like ours beneath the earth,
Just how much, if anything will it be worth?

We all needed to go and register our land,
And in town we reached up to the bright stars,
As the dreams of riches which we had planned,
Has come; happily true and all this oil of ours.
Our farming life was badly fraught with fear,
Because the, oil badly pollutes the soil here.

We were unkempt dirty and looked dirt poor,
But we tried to find an expert for their advice,
And after knocking on many an expert's door,
We concluded that no expert could we entice.
Could it be that our dirty and tardy appearance,
Or perhaps it is also a slight bit of incoherence.

I bumped into a young girl, who was in tears,
She came out of some offices very fast,
She nearly knocked me over as it appears,
We caught up with her when she stopped at last.
I asked what the matter was and who made her cry,
It's my boss he pinches my bottom always on the sly.

Junior Surveyor

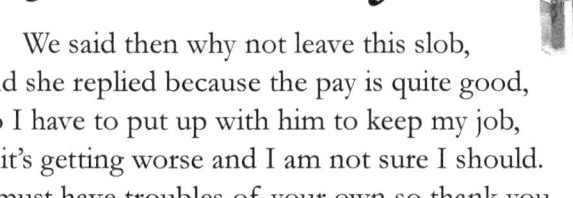

We said then why not leave this slob,
And she replied because the pay is quite good,
So I have to put up with him to keep my job,
But it's getting worse and I am not sure I should.
You must have troubles of your own so thank you,
I said, "We need a surveyor for an oil breakthrough".

Her eyes lit up like bright diamonds in the sky,
She said you are not joking are you, you guys,
We told her about the mine, what we saw and why,
But without a surveyor we will have no prize.
She said, "Won't be legal without a proper claim,
I said, "We had a claim but no surveyor all the same".

"I am a junior surveyor with a good grade,
And claims need to be looked at by a legal mind,
So I suggest you check the claim you have made,
And I will help you by surveying your find".
We went to the mine and she took samples of oil,
She paid to have checks of fluid and even soil.

She said, "I have a living wage so I will pay,
For a solicitor to check clauses on your claim,
The chemical tests done in an independent way,
And see you do not get excited about fame.
You must only speak about what I say,
Then if this is good I will want more than pay".

The young college girl said she would agree,
To be legally our geographical surveyor,
And she said that she would do this work for free,
But in return she wanted to be a player.
With the right qualifications from university,
She said that we could be really big in the city.

Value if any?

A surveyor, but she is only a young girl in jeans,
However we told her all about our enterprise,
She tried to value it and the construction scenes,
And, told us never to sell this plot or compromise.
To find out the amount of oil and its value,
We needed a person clearly honest and true.

The young girl's name is Leslie and we were glad,
That for a small percentage she will advise,
But what is a percentage and will it be so bad,
And Leslie so young can she be all that wise.
I thought why she is not at home with her Mum,
But perhaps girls in town are not so dumb.

Leslie came back with very good news,
She had had the results of the chemical tests,
She said, "It is of high grade and not to lose,
By giving to carpet bagging bids by pests.
We will go and see our solicitor friend,
And draw up a contract to keep at his end.

The legal advisor doubled his usual fee,
But Leslie knocked him down and explained,
Where the solicitor wanted afterwards to be,
And that was having some of what was gained.
Leslie said that he has friends in the city,
And with good prices we will be sitting pretty.

We were unsure but we trusted Leslie,
She said there may be more than the claim bears,
And that she wanted to do more tests and see,
And look at some ecology maps and books of hers.
She spoke in terms which we did not understand,
But we concluded that things would be quite grand.

Progressive Differences

After her second lot of tests were complete,
And the maps and books she had put away,
Then in her car the solicitor we went to meet,
With the prospect of where a bigger lake lay.
Neil the solicitor housed us and bought us clothes,
Then for us all to go out for a meal he chose.

From many underground rivers and lakes,
Oil is pumped up our highly productive wells,
And sold by the barrel at the highest stakes,
Leslie negotiates the top price providing the product sells.
Fortunately for us Leslie, our partner, is clever,
Geologically, financially and as determined as ever!

We felt excited at the prospect of more oil,
She had an idea of more claims we should make,
But would mean much research and toil,
By all of us to, have a much bigger stake.
Geologically it could be twice as much still,
Depending on the quality and depth of the drill.

Then Neil and Leslie came back quite late,
They were not speaking so what was badly wrong,
So I said, "It is time to talk in a frank debate,
This was bound to happen before very long".
You are working but you will not always agree,
There are always differences in some degree.

Leslie said, "He badly humiliated me,
He questioned my judgement on the oil grade,
Bankers, surveyors and oil buyers sadly,
All believe his masculine and legal charade".
I said, "And because you are just a young girl,
They believed him as things began to unfurl"?

Prospects of Administration

He agreed it was only an average grade,
"When it is not and you can prove our claim,
But why when there is money to be made,
And we want Neil's side just the same.
The buyer said it was only average grade,
And the bankers want at least the interest paid.

Land claims, state surveys, chartered deeds,
Machinery like pumps, drills and gauges,
Registry Office and tax status code has needs,
And lastly the matter of the employee's wages.
So we have a million pound debt to our name,
And a bank, that wants money all the same.

We should see the Chairman for his views,
The bank may, employ surveyors of their own,
To back up Leslie's findings and then choose,
But now we need to sell and loose but not moan.
I want to be able to pay half of the interest,
With a hundred, barrels a day at the best.

We all agreed and wanted to know more,
Neil said I have bought five drills up until now,
The next four must each be a prosperous bore,
Nine month's money is all the bank will allow.
The bank may agree to lend us more in May,
By then the drilling results might come our way.

At present land and labour are relatively cheap,
Paying by dollars, our hard working employees,
Is popular with them and we hope it will keep,
But charges might come for changing policies.
I mean if the government insists on the Rand,
We have to know now where we will stand.

Loans and Progress

Three months later in May we have five drills,
With over nine hundred barrels per day,
Neil and Leslie were friends again but with no frills,
At thirty two dollars per barrel was for us was OK.
To the buyer the Bank Chairman said, "Go or stay,
But the price is thirty two dollars per barrel today".

Before banking the Bank Chairman was in oil,
And he saw a chance for us and for the bank,
So that the government does not try to foil,
Many more of our wells being successfully sank.
With half a million dollars more on our loan,
We have ten more productive wells to clone.

Leslie was working on even more sites,
There was twenty miles of barren beach and sea,
So Neil put in a legal claim for the oil rites,
And enquired as to how much an oil rig might be.
The cost was truly staggering I must admit,
But it was in our portfolio and within our remit.

It was not thought then that ladies could trade,
We each have ten percent of this rich claim,
And between us a vast fortune we have all made,
And many employees are happy just the same.
But we came from hungry dirt farmers before,
And Leslie was a young student and she was poor.

The Chinese have built docks within this time space,
To accommodate four average size oil tankers,
They have put a terminal as if it were a race,
And Neil spoke enquiringly to our bankers.
China wants oil not claims, drills, rather than deeds,
They want oil fast but they have great needs.

More Drills

Ten more drills now the bankers advised,
With a further twenty in six months time,
With three miles of the terminal he surmised,
Build your own pipeline larger, sublime.
We will tell the Chinese we have lots of oil to pour,
Let them know potentially what is in store.

With ten drills in only two months we sold,
One point seven two eight million dollars,
Of oil and the banker's proposal was quite bold,
And we thought we were still relatively scholars.
You can have a hundred million dollars to purchase,
Docks, a terminal more drills and shipping space.

Also buy oil tankers, oil rigs and faster pumps,
Speeding up the pumps if you possibly can,
Here speak to this man from "About Oil Slumps",
Leslie was uneasy but we all listened to the man.
I work in Solar Power and Britain leads the way,
Solar pumps cost nothing to run with a power ray.

We can install and maintain them for you,
But I must warn that they can be too fast,
Between thirty and seventy per cent might do,
As I believe you have ten more wells a last.
We said yes by the Chinese oil terminal store,
Let me see the size of your pipes inner core.

Twenty inch pipes should do alright,
See that they are maintained every ten weeks,
We are learning about oil by a leading solar light,
What or who is next and what if it peaks.
Leslie was sure of the quantity in our wells,
And said, "I can not foresee any alarm bells".

British Solar Pumps

Thirty million pound the solar pumps cost,
I look forward to see if it was worth it or not,
If not can we pay off the interest we have lost,
We can not complain but that will be their lot.
A million pounds each is stretching our budget a bit,
But I am sure the bank can accommodate it.

Within another three months, by May,
Thirty new large oil wells have been drilled,
And the solar pumps reserve energy by day,
So that the dark night shift has been filled.
Three hundred and sixty dollars each day,
Was making, it hard to keep the Chinese at bay.

We were building another forty oil wells,
Twenty each side of terminal and docks,
For pumping quickly without gassy smells,
From our oil wells to our terminal stocks!
Then to the petrol refinery or to an oil tanker,
But we have to stop pumping for an anchor.

We paid twenty million off our bank loan,
But thirty million might leave us a bit short,
Five million dollars was interest alone,
But what was the total cost of our port?
Forty dollars per barrel the Chinese will pay,
India forty two if we ship it their way.

We spoke, with the bank chairman who said,
"I will hold your port to secure a further loan,
And place a further eighty million ahead,
Because your, company is quite well known.
Neil contacted Dave about solar pumps galore,
And said, "We need forty maybe many more".

Chinese Interest

The work was now going particularly well,
Neil and Leslie were quiet and a bit remote,
So I said to them what is the matter please tell,
Well nothing now we have tankers afloat.
It has nothing to do with work try me again,
Leslie and I need to stay focused in the main.

You give too many people too much latitude,
The banker could call in the loan very soon,
And take our port away if he were in the mood,
Then sell it to the Chinese at a huge profit any day.
The Chinese will keep tankers and remain,
But on a license the government might abstain.

Why would the South African government refuse?
Because with Health and Safety they don't care,
The South African workers rights they abuse,
And if a spill occurs dirt would be left there.
"Does the South African government know"?
I asked but China just seems to grow and grow.

With the forty more wells we were doing fine,
In fact it was close to a million dollars a day,
So in just six months Leslie and Neil did shine,
Neil announced, "No more debts for us to pay".
We all cheered and Leslie kissed Neil,
Then I think she wondered, "What does he feel".

"Five rigs now," she said to change the subject,
"Long rigs in less than two hundred feet,
With special faster solar pumps anyone object,
And it would put us with the giants and the elite".
Neil said, "But the pipes might be six miles,
Should we not first do two as just trials"?

Oil Rig Pipelines

One is as close to our refinery as can be,
And churns out seven hundred barrels per day,
Which we sell as petroleum very profitably,
And an American tanker comes into our bay.
Tankers will run aground without any doubt,
If the, water is not deep enough there about.

The other oil rig's pipeline goes six miles out,
Tankers fill up and on the Indian market it sells,
The Chinese do not like us spreading it about,
And have asked to dig forty more wells.
We consulted Leslie who said, "I have in store,
Space to dig twenty five wells possibly more".

We told the Chinese it would be twenty five,
And the reply was it is forty or none,
So Leslie said, "Then no more will arrive,
I have done my research what have you done"?
The Chinese were adamant but they soon returned,
And said, "Can we help we are concerned".

"We can have twenty five wells more operating,
But about three months they will take,
And there are five large lakes by my calculating,
And they are twelve miles away but all in our stake.
I have estimated that there could be for each lake,
Could your terminal handle this potential intake"?

Leslie went on to say "From the twenty five,
We can expect seven thousand barrels per day,
But from the five lakes it will need a better drive,
So there may be quite some delay.
But in future twenty thousand barrels more,
Can your terminal take that score"?

Faster Solar Pumps Needed

The Chinese look puzzled and said, "Yes",
Then Leslie said, "It would be twice the size,
At least possibly more please don't guess,
A wrong estimate would not be wise.
Strong pumps to pump up the oil we need,
And five pumps along the pipeline to succeed".

Leslie was happy and her happiness had that appeal,
We needed to contact the Solar Pump man,
So we went and explained the situation to Neil,
I said, "Cheer up Neil now go and kiss her man".
He looked at me in a strange sort of way,
But he did as he was told and made her day.

The Solar Man, Dave came within a fortnight,
We put a sixty million dollar order in his hand,
With another order if the power was alright,
For twenty million for where more rigs stand.
The Chinese built another terminal for our oil,
To save disorder, spillage, delays and more toil.

In six months the Chinese were paying about,
Nine hundred thousand dollars per day,
The Americans pay half a million no doubt,
And half a million comes from India's way.
America spends four hundred thousand as a, rule,
Buying; from our refinery our industrial fuel.

This is nearly two million dollars per day,
Paying off our debts and feeling no pain,
Five more rigs would take India a long way,
To pay six hundred thousand dollars is plain.
The totals now are about two point four,
Million dollars and triple our refinery's score.

Insurance and Currency

Banker Jim and Solar man Dave,
Made an appointment to see us right away,
Explained what South Africa wants to save,
Because a, coastline would destroy their day.
He said if the Chinese or Indians come to drill,
Or Americans then their oil might just spill.

It was explained that they wouldn't compensate,
They have not got the experts either to clean,
So the government has refused to contemplate,
Saying like, releasing a beast that is not at all green.
The Chinese have offered to bring in Renminbi Yuan,
It is the second currency and nobody else can.

First is the US Dollar do we all agree,
Then second and well behind is the EU's euro,
The third most traded is the Japanese yen you see,
And fourth is Pound Sterling you would know.
The fifth most traded currency is the Swiss Franc,
Now the Australian Dollar is demoted to sixth rank.

The Canadian Dollar is strong and seventh in line,
Joint eighth is the Hong Kong Dollar and South African Rand,
China's currency, the renminbi Yuan is doing just fine,
The Yuan like the Chinese economy is going to expand.
South Africa trades with the commonwealth most,
So many dollars from African countries Britain will host.

Of the most traded currencies this is really somewhere,
The Yuan finally trades in Germany, but not the US or Japan?
Last year it came to Britain but trade then was only fair,
So for this to be more traded make it work the best we can.
The Rand like the Yuan does exchange in, Hong Kong,
And about New York and Tokyo is something wrong?

Business Expansion

The banker, Jim explained all to him,
But what the ministers actually do,
We give to each dirty power on a whim,
Or will he say for them there is nothing new.
He does not want them always at the ready,
But he wants to keep the economy steady.

We were given twice as much more land,
We now pay tax and so do the Indians and US,
Who are building their own docks that are grand,
So they are happy and there will be no mess.
We as a company are well insured for any spill,
Not that we expect a bad leak, pipe or drill.

Within another six months they were ready,
We had surveyed the land and built many pipes,
And soon all of us were going quite steady,
And after all the debts there were many gripes.
It is only one billion dollars complained Neil,
I wondered is that complaint really real.

We were assured that next year we would net,
At least three billion dollars perhaps even more,
With Leslie's explorers more targets will be met,
And Jim was thinking of a business non core.
Half a Billion dollars how could it be used best,
And in British Solar, Power we decided to invest.

Dave was very grateful and checked our pumps,
And he managed to speed them up quite a lot,
Now money was coming in great big clumps,
So Jim the banker bought us a large yacht.
He bought Sterling, Australian Dollars and Rand,
As well as British and Australian Bonds as planned.

Solar Business too

I have good news said Dave the Solar Man,
That the solar pumps were selling very well,
The solar energy we are fitting as fast as we can,
And other products we have designed will sell.
We could sell products that are solar and clean,
Many types of dishwasher and washing machine.

Vacuums and fans would make us much more,
With many industrial and many domestic kind,
With the right investment there is money for sure,
These new domestic appliances are a rich find.
We even hope to go and produce motorcars,
Vans, trucks, trains and reach to the stars.

We said, "Your Solar could quickly expand,
And two billion dollars would buy us a part,
He looked uneasy as if he did not understand,
I will get my lawyers and they can make a start.
We own 48% of the company as a whole,
But for company voting rights we have no role.

The Solar Company flourished in the US and China,
Providing energy for industry and people's homes,
Their appliances are powerful and none are finer,
We have samples courtesy of Dave Soames.
The car and truck industry was practically complete,
But it surely could not make oil and gas obsolete?

The last chapter of this story would be to tell,
That they are very much in love Leslie and Neil,
They are starry eyed and under quite a spell,
So I said to Neil tell her how you feel.
He said soon it will be legal and bells will ring,
For Leslie and Neil happiness it will bring.

African Big Game

The African Big Game was coined after safaris on foot,
By white hunters pursuing the continent's Big Five,
The Lion, African Elephant, Leopard, Rhinoceros but,
Also the Cape Buffalo if that species can survive.
Fortunately Africa now has laws to protect Big Game,
But crime and unscrupulous acts happen all the same.

The Chital, the Zebra, the Giraffe and the Wildebeest,
Are in great numbers but they are always sought,
By many carnivores to provide them with a feast,
But that is, only if they are slow enough to get caught.
They have strong legs and can usually run clear,
And of being an endangered species, they do not fear.

The herbivore young are mostly born strong and well,
Not just Chital, Zebra, Giraffe and the Wildebeest,
But also the Hares, the Antelope and the Gazelle,
All with strong family ties, to survive the winter at least.
These animals have not suffered any great reduction,
Because, of a good family life and healthy reproduction.

These four legged herbivores are all fair Game,
Each day for Lions, Leopards and Cheetahs as food,
But with sophisticated aids it is just not the same,
As man will kill for sport, trespass and man will intrude.
The chance of something escaping man is slim,
In contrast a carnivore's chances are particularly grim.

If a Lion, a Cheetah or a Leopard comes their way,
The herd will split up and run to stay alive,
The predator's appetite may be satisfied anyway,
By catching an animal, that could not, survive.
Cheetahs can turn and run at eighty miles per hour,
But this speed cannot be sustained with its limited power.

African Carnivores

The Lion is the largest carnivore of course,
And as such Lions command a great deal of respect,
So they growl fiercely as a show of their force,
And they can set a wealth of power to great effect.
The Lion lives a carefree life with his family in a pride,
Because except for man; all other animals scurry and hide.

For many days and many miles a Leopard can stalk,
Hoping for a herd of Zebra and for some luck,
Trying for the weak and injured that can hardly walk,
Or be quick enough to catch a young Chital buck.
Leopards have the stealth, patience and the will,
To, wait many days before making a kill.

Hyenas are the second largest of the carnivores,
But they are lazy and quite slow on their feet,
Although they have big teeth and very strong jaws,
They need to have a carcass to tear up, into food, to eat.
The Hyena is the largest African scavenger of all,
And the smell of dead meat is a very arousing call.

Wild Dogs hunt in packs and Vultures will fly,
Jackals also scavenge and hunt for small prey,
Like rodents or hares, Vultures pluck from the sky,
And such scavengers feed on carrion in their own way.
A piece of dying Gazelle, Antelope or Hare,
Will make a tasty meal for whoever is first there.

The hunter, the hunted and the scavenger I have portrayed,
But man, the sportsman, is different in every way,
Because he hunts but not for food he just likes to raid,
So any herbivore, carnivore or scavenger he might slay.
A native man hunting for food with a large spear,
Might get lucky if an Antelope were to, appear!

Accidental Win

This win was so totally and utterly unexpected,
My wife and I had luck, which we could barely believe,
That from so many people we had actually been selected,
For this, well-organised, glorious, luxury break to receive.
Like most people we had never won anything before,
Least of all did we expect a prize from a prize draw.

We had tickets to go to Liverpool Street station,
So in this London station a chauffeur met us there,
And drove us in luxury to our accommodation,
Which was a five star hotel and the BBC Centre was near.
The food was special and nothing went wrong,
It is part of Langham International Hong Kong.

In London, my wife and I had a good fortune spent,
This weekend in a select but very comfortable hotel,
With all thanks due to General Accident,
Because we were happy and treated extremely well.
Because of all the famous places I had to drop a rhyme,
Thanking you so much for such a romantic time.

We saw Regent Street and Trafalgar Square,
Bond Street, Whitehall and Horse Guard's Parade,
St James Park and the admiralty buildings there,
Buckingham Palace and their luxury tourist trade!
We never saw the London Underground,
And there is much more to see next time around.

We had stayed at The Langham Hilton Hotel,
Fond memories of London we will always redeem,
Of important historical places that we now know so well,
And also of General Accident's great esteem.
We went as guests to some of the elite nightspots,
Like the West End to see 'Grease' and Ronnie Scott's.

Kingfisher Is

I am good-looking and the world's prettiest bird,
I have on show a beautiful booming red breast,
And my unique plumage is so pleasantly flared,
So I stand out from the dull feathers of the rest.
I live by the river where it is quiet and remote,
Where, I can parade my red breast and dark blue coat.

I am a residential bird not a migratory bird,
I love the gushing water where I live all year,
And going somewhere else to me is quite absurd,
Because I will, stay a permanent resident here.
Each day I will catch fish nourishment for my diet,
From any natural river or pond that is clean and quiet.

I can perch quietly on the branch of a strong tree,
From where I can dive into the water like a bullet,
And catch a tasty fish without much difficulty,
Then I would turn my fish to face my gullet.
If I did not or could not turn my fish first,
Then I, the Kingfisher would come off the worst.

My nest is always inside a small crack or hole,
Well hidden in the bank of a river or a pond,
My mate and I furnish it well on the whole,
So my mate and our chicks can live well and bond.
We live in this wild rustic, peaceful embrace,
That has good fish and is the perfect upmarket place.

When our habitation drastically changes,
Like in the winter of nineteen sixty two,
Our population dropped and will take ages,
Because building and reproducing we both need to do.
Forestation grows when the weather gets milder,
But river routes may change and nests get wilder.

Kingfisher Community

The pale blue sky stretches up high overhead,
To celebrate a beautiful, sunny and placid day,
When everything comes alive to pop out its head,
To rejoice, to sing, to dance and to play!
If a cloud bursts and it starts to pour with rain,
Mud might flood in and soak our nest again.

Climate change affects our nests and our chicks,
River water can wet our chicks and cause a flood,
Then we have to rebuild using mud and sticks,
While our chicks will fare the best they could.
My chicks and mate need to live in a burrow of clay,
They need to learn early of things we do each day.

Little is known about how us Kingfishers court,
Reproduction plays a large part in our life,
Of which human knowledge is sorely fraught,
So, human anger on Kingfishers is rife.
So with enemies like nature and man,
Kingfishers dodge the bullets the best we can.

Each one of our fine chicks now needs to learn,
The essential facts to guide them through their life,
Like when feeding, the fish they must always turn,
Which means head first, otherwise choking is rife.
We taught fishing, flying and finding a nest,
These are the essentials for their ultimate test.

We hope that they will be competent and mature,
Recognise their enemies or they might die,
Choose a handsome mate and reproduce still more,
And always beware of dangers from the rivers and the sky.
Life is a learning curve each and every day,
So try to stay safe and avoid the ultimate penalty.

Annual Family Holiday

I have really not shown my full appreciation,
For what my loving parents did every single year,
By providing us with a good holiday as recreation,
So all our family have many memories to hold dear.
Holidays mean washing trouble, packing and strain,
Then dragging our suitcases; from train to train.

When finally my Dad got a small family motor car,
Our holidays were less hectic and easier to do,
In fact in one day we could pack and go very far,
Being a bit older and more comfortable too!
If only half the journey was made we would stay,
Overnight bed and breakfast as a, pleasant delay.

After breakfast we would go to the best beach,
When I was young I made sandcastles in the sand,
But when I grew older football I would teach,
To my little brothers who thought that I was grand.
We all played on the hard sand when Dad came,
And we always had a thrilling and exciting game.

Whilst on the hard sand playing exciting football,
Mum would hold Jane on for a wobbly donkey ride,
Because Jane was small and might so easily fall,
And this all had to be done with the incoming tide.
When the tide is coming in then for a swim we will go,
But when the tide ebbs, wet sand and pools start to show.

At midday we all sat and ate a packed lunch each,
Everything was always very carefully planned,
Including a primus stove to make tea on the beach,
Milk in a, big Thermos and Typhoo tea on the stand.
In the afternoon iced lollies were a special treat,
Then speechless with our lollies we sat there to eat.

Value for Money

To enjoy ourselves we did exactly as we please,
That is providing what we do is safe for us three,
All of us have skin that seems to burn with ease,
Especially when we are just coming; out of the sea.
Dad was an extremely good swimmer you can tell,
And he taught the rest of us how to swim as well.

When I say, "us three" I mean my brothers and I,
Often my Mum and Dad would go off with Jane,
For a rest and a drink in a pub with a meat pie,
Because us boys not Jane were then quite a pain.
Having a good suntan was really only a dream,
Despite all the heat and rubbing on all that sun cream.

Sometimes it would start to drizzle or even rain,
We would stay there, if the rain were only slight,
Have a ride on the ferry, the tram or the train,
But shelter until the rain stops and it is again bright.
We all have fun on different rides at the fun fair,
We three laughed but Jane was very easy to scare.

In years to come holiday camps were the best,
And if it rains we could always play indoors,
Table tennis, snooker or have a drink and rest,
And some holiday camps would lay on tours.
These holiday camps spread out into France,
With cheap Virgin Airways if one gets a chance.

Soon also to Spain, Germany, Italy and the US,
Places that only rich Britons could afford,
So from German domination we have to progress,
But it was a German who takes the final holiday award.
The Germans stopped occupying all the deckchairs,
Instead they dominated holiday prices and airfares.

Eating Chinese

The Princess Gardens is where we often dine,
It is a Chinese restaurant where you can stay,
To eat fresh sea fish that is cooked just fine,
While drinking chilled but delicious Chardonnay.
Many people who go there eat, drink but do not drive,
They get a taxi home so that they will survive.

This Chinese restaurant is one of Mr. Tso's,
Whose specialities are fresh seafood and fish,
Cooked on the bone and if you choose,
Filleted to, leave just white meat on your dish.
He goes to the fish market as early as he can,
To buy fresh fish for his restaurant's cooking pan.

If you do not have soup, have crispy seaweed,
There are many dishes of Lobster and of Sea Bass,
A comprehensive menu for Mr. Tso to succeed,
Although his Steamed Dover Sole is, top of my class.
A waiter comes to your table and will cut away,
With surgical precision all the bones that inlay.

The menu has Chinese banquets by the score,
To suit almost everybody's taste and appetite,
So why not come to eat here or at least to explore,
Some of their special, courses for your, sheer delight.
Many recipes are from the Provinces of China,
So in England the banquets can be much finer.

Some delicious starters are on the menu,
But if you have prawn cocktail for an appetiser,
And a large main meal then a dessert you not pursue,
Because when your stomach is full it is much wiser.
The desserts are usually with contents like cream,
And often they are more fattening than they might seem.

My Favourite Dishes

Sweet and sour chicken or sweet and sour pork,
Are sweet and nutritious dishes that appeal to kids,
Because this kind of dish one can eat with a fork,
But it is something that a vegetarian forbids.
Sweet and sour foods go with fried or boiled rice,
Although some people always think chips are nice.

Crispy duck is a particular favourite of mine,
With pancakes, cucumber, and hoi sin sauce,
And the dark meat rolled to make a design,
That one can eat out of one's hand of course.
A quarter of crispy duck can make a man a feast,
Providing your, appetite has not greatly increased.

A sizzling platter comes in a cast iron dish,
Laid in a wooden stand to withstand the heat,
In a sauce or gravy in fact anything you wish,
And on the platter are all your greens and meat.
Beef is common but so are pork and lamb,
And boiled rice as a side dish you would summon.

With tasty traditional English food you will find,
A portfolio of cooking and food that will appeal,
So it is difficult to make up your hungered mind,
Which, traditional dish, you want for your meal.
The next important decision now of course,
Is to, choose a complimentary gravy or sauce.

Then to add to their quality of service and food,
There are classic spirits, wines and champagne,
Or other such beverages that may suit your mood,
And you will return here again and again.
Good timing and happiness combine to complete,
An evening out dining that is a welcome treat.

Ocean World

I am Charlie and I am an infamous Blue Whale,
The oceans and the seas are vast and sometimes deep,
So I can tell you many a true story or a very tall tale,
Of secret hiding places that whales like I must keep.
I am a mammal so need to breathe to stay alive,
But when gruesome lurks I fear I must dive.

I am the biggest animal but I am gentle and kind,
I have never done the human race any harm,
But only beneath the sea or ocean is where I find,
That life for me will be timeless, tranquil and calm.
We are not children however we live in schools,
Adhere strictly to family values and all its rules.

Our predecessors were all big and very much like me,
Large animals like us do not usually eat meat,
Because in the clean ocean, or the blue sea,
There is so much else we can choose to eat.
I devour about eight tons of krill each day,
And some other small pelagic animals, this way.

I am by far the biggest animal on our planet of all,
That is not just at present it means of all time,
Because I am very long, very wide and very tall,
But the human race thinks that this is a crime.
We are very big, but we are harmless and shy,
You hunt us and kill us but can you tell me why?

In fact I weigh about one hundred and forty ton,
From my head to my fin is about one hundred feet,
In Summer I migrate to the Arctic, out of the sun,
Because Blue Whales like me cannot stand the heat.
More than six hundred feet down is too steep,
So I dive down no further than the semi deep.

I am a Gentle Giant

I have very sensitive and very acute hearing,
So the noise that a launch or a motorboat will make,
Leaves me confused and unsteady, often fearing,
That a large sonic boom will follow in its wake.
Motorboats drink petrol from a small metal tank,
And they speed humans on this dirty wooden plank.

It is only <u>man</u> who really frightens the likes of me,
Few creatures can so much as badly dent my hide,
In places where the water is so warm I would never be,
I mean swamps where Crocodiles and Alligators reside.
The extinct Dinosaur reptiles had amour that was grand,
But they could only move slowly and across land.

Most Sharks are fast, have big teeth and a dorsal fin,
They like very shallow water and the shore close by,
Whereas I like the cold, wide and deep ocean to be in,
With a cool desert wind and a bright, blue sky.
Sharks very rarely go near Wales,
And never to, Scotland or our Norwegian trails.

It is not as if we Whales destroy or steal man's turf,
Take away their food or attack viciously their young,
Because we all live and eat well beneath the surf,
In deep, vast oceans that are very widely flung.
Our habitat should be away from man's empire,
Yet we still find ourselves well in the line of fire!

We are still wanted by these primates without hair,
Who ride on their powerful majestic metal steed,
And they fire explosive teeth through the air,
Which are tied to ropes whilst our bodies bleed!
With men and their steeds that cause such pollution,
We are now in a state of constant dilution.

Public Transport on Time

Public transport was mostly on time then,
But that was long before we had traffic jams,
It was provided basically for the working men,
In the form of double-decker horse, drawn trams.
These basic trams adopted a pollution free pose,
And their manure fed many a fine looking rose.

Industry was, and still does, wait for no man,
Next came trams that had an engine instead of a horse,
So when the quicker electrically-powered trams began,
The fleets of them were driven very hard of course.
The Green Goddesses had a wire on the roof section,
That powered the new trams from an overhead connection.

Not long after traffic on the road greatly increased,
With cars and buses having tyres and not a track,
So when buses came the demand for trams decreased,
Being quicker, easily-produced buses never looked back.
The buses and cars use the internal combustion engine,
That exhales smoke and dirt into the air we live in.

The first revolutionary buses gave a bumpy ride,
And upstairs mostly, working men would smoke,
There was also a bar for to jump on at the backside,
And collecting each man's fare was really no joke.
There was a driver to drive each double-decker bus,
And a conductor to collect the fares without; any fuss.

The new Atlantian bus drivers operated the front door,
Where passengers boarding would pay their fare,
So progress saw no need for conductors anymore,
As the, drivers could do their job from where they were.
Opposite the door is where the driver always stayed,
And the doors meant that journeys were safety weighed.

Power-assisted steering

With power-assisted steering, these buses were the best,
And they could turn corners with a cut and thrust,
So that most of the public would be put through a test,
Of endurance to show that these buses you can trust.
Seventy seven passengers these buses would seat,
And the independent suspension was a real treat.

All double-decker buses have now faded into the night,
For a more spacious and cleaner single-decker one,
That is safer for people when they board or alight,
Like elderly people or those not so able getting on.
For wheelchairs and prams, space it will afford,
Its platform will lower for people to get on board.

In most modern cities electric trams are back too,
Single-decker ones that were specially designed,
And if people use them, traffic jams will be few,
But our great public transport is a minority of a kind.
Car owners should have extra Council Tax to pay,
As the council, has to maintain, the Queen's highway.

All electronic trams are the environment's friends,
So it is only cars and lorries that damage each town,
But knowing how we are transported by such trends,
Even, if it gives our homes and roads a dirty down.
A clean ecosystem is a fight needing to be fought,
So too are travelling times, speed, safety and comfort.

The old Green Goddesses are still in action,
Now fifty years on and many still run like new,
Mostly at resorts as a seaside town attraction,
Or in a museum for the, young and old to view.
Our Public Transport system is said to be in decay,
But it has stood the test of time and is still here today.

Hot House

In April melons and sweet corn can be grown,
Much water will they both need,
Pruning greenhouse climbers can also be sown,
And they can hog the sun just out of pure greed.
Remove dead fronds, spray and give us peat,
Because often your labours are still not complete.

Many plants in the spring are sown from pots,
Many houseplants have been grown from seed,
They grow to cheerful plants that have their lots,
Each one is a different size, shape and breed.
Some come as bulbs and others are leafy shoots,
Even cuttings but they must all have firm roots.

I, the melon will ripen when am a good size,
I will come off the stem easily when I am ready,
I am tasty but do not rush me guys,
And don't pull me if the stem is not steady.
By pressing a sweet corn's kernel with a fingernail,
One can tell that in Great Britain it will fail.

I have a leafy, spiral, stem that is not thick,
And I grow my best in an extremely humid heat,
As tomatoes will need the strong support of a stick,
So I can grow well in fine sand, lime and peat.
In the Summer in a greenhouse I will do fine,
As I am healthy, I flourish, blossom and shine.

We are often grown in a greenhouse from seeds,
Then watered, nurtured and very well protected,
But always kept away from destructive weeds,
And to a stick, we are usually tied or connected.
My fruit at first is only small and green,
But when the sun shines a yellow skin will be seen.

Humid Atmosphere

This greenhouse needs to have constant heat,
So my small green fruits can begin to grow,
Then begin to ripen soon to become complete,
But some of them drop and to the ground they go.
I need so much attention paid each and every day,
And the dead fruit at my stem must be moved away.

The cucumber is another plant that is grown alone,
They are greenhouse residents, who are inferior,
In fact they need protective glass tubes of their own,
And they are long and thin with a green exterior.
Bearing such artificial aids they can not be well,
And if it is infectious how can we tell.

Their surrounding tubes are such an excess weight,
That, thick wires have to hold them to take the strain,
And their fruit grows along the tube fairly straight,
But of course the poor dears must be in great pain.
Tomatoes and cucumbers have weighty fruits,
And they are often tasty if not willing recruits.

Greenhouse fruits when plucked in their prime,
And organic vegetables grown in beds of soil,
Can all this be eaten within a very short time,
Or will they need refrigerating and wrapped in foil?
As a summation one could find it tasty to eat,
With lettuce, cress, radish and some cold meat.

Of our pristine fruits we are always relieved,
They are usually washed and put on a plate,
So that a salutary salad lunch can be achieved,
And such summer lunches man can often create.
Cucumber sandwiches too, I believe were born,
For sunny days of cricket being, played on the lawn.

Corgi

I am a Pembrokeshire Corgi, a native of Wales,
And despite me living near Tenby on a dirty farm,
My charm and personal charisma never pales,
Herding smelly cattle and keeping them all calm.
The American owner has an odd foreign drawl,
He speaks no Welsh and can not speak English well at all.

Unless I am extremely ill, I am up with the lark,
Then I will go to the kitchen to get myself fed,
But the kitchen then is usually very cold and dark,
As the sun's light there has not yet been shed.
I start each working day very much the same,
Herding the fat cows, who are quite tame!

My short legs sprint spryly into a grassy field,
Where docile looking Jersey cows are stood,
With many churns of creamy milk yet to yield,
Each cow bows its head and now chews the cud.
I gently nip their fleshy heels to let them know,
That to the parlour it is time for them to go.

I believe that the hardest of all my daily chores,
Is to keep the girls still, that is, all in one pack,
And by using my mouth and being on all fours,
I manage to guide them precisely into the shack.
Once inside the shack, women pull their teats,
They pull them so hard the cows must be in pleats.

If anybody went to pull on my family jewels,
Then they would feel how hard my teeth can bite,
Soon blood would be scattered into deep dark pools,
Until, the villain is unconscious or out of sight.
If anybody dared to give me such pain,
They would get much more than a look of disdain.

Knowing One's Place

I drink a lot of water each and every day,
And a bowl of water is kept fresh for me as a rule,
Although milk sometimes comes my way,
I know where milk comes from so it is not so cool.
The old man I believe is the salt of the earth,
He gives me water because he knows my true worth.

We have a few unwritten rules about where I live,
One is that even if I can reach I will not steal,
Coffee tables are low and the old man will forgive,
For leaving tasty morsels that I would like to feel.
I am disciplined and will sit there in pain,
While my lips, are licked time and time again.

If food is on the floor then no dispute; it is mine,
Like a thick piece of fillet steak medium raw,
Is especially tasty and will suit me really fine,
In the entire house are the sheds to the back door.
The girls are quick but not really that desperate,
But the old man is in a totally different state.

At the old man you will often hear me growl,
My territory is the floor and I have first choice,
He often picks up his dish and gives me a scowl,
In fact I bet he would eat pig food and then rejoice.
I am too quick for him although he is often fast,
And he has challenged me many times in the past.

This creamy cow's milk then goes into a churn,
And later it is taken somewhere to be pasteurised too,
But all the hungry cows now I have to return,
Into a lush green field of juicy, grass for them to chew.
I always have to escort these cows twice a day,
So when I am not doing this I am asleep or at play.

Seven Liverpools

There are three small Liverpools in America,
One is in Texas; another is in New York State,
There is a third Liverpool town in Pennsylvania,
And a forth one sprung up in Ohio at a later date.
Three were built just before the British Empire fell,
They are all like trading posts; about that size as well.

Three bigger Liverpools important in their own way,
One is a city in New South Wales, Australia,
Another is a city in the Canadian port in Liverpool Bay,
And independently these countries have not been a failure.
The original Liverpool in Merseyside is the best,
And it was built about 500 years before the rest.

Liverpool in New South Wales near Sydney,
Has a population of just over twenty one thousand,
Over fifty five per cent are not from that country,
It is on the Georges River and was agricultural land.
Liverpool was founded in eighteen ten as a settlement,
But in the nineteen sixties urbanism is contentment.

In England, there is a city that was born for gentry,
It was built by King John, who built a large castle,
And he decided to deploy many a fine sentry,
To ensure that in this city there was no hassle.
Liverpool was started with monks in the 12th Century;
From a small peasant settle by the Mersey Estuary.

In August 2007, Liverpool was 800 years old,
As Liverpool received its Charter to become a city,
Officially in 1207 but businessmen already were bold,
And Liverpool will prosper, I hope to eternity.
This city was mainly for seafarers and ports,
But such a cosmopolitan people have skills of all sorts.

Merseyside's Liverpool

Whereas if one looks to the Mersey's other side,
You will see pirate ships come into sheltered coves,
Bringing with them their plundered booty to hide,
Such as, rum, drugs and rich treasure troves.
Pirate ships were unchecked and have no ties,
So they came and went until Customs and Excise.

Liverpool was very rich and the greatest port,
Because of rich merchants trading their wares,
But now the jet age sees less freight is brought,
And Liverpool the port is poorer but nobody cares.
With much determination, struggle and strife,
Liverpool will change to again rejuvenate its life.

From their huge successes made from trade,
Businessmen had cultural artefacts to donate,
Buildings, statues and machines were made,
To, recognise this innovative and cultural date.
Now wealth and prosperity it has no more,
But it's cultural heritage is filled to the core.

With talented musicians of style and class,
Liverpool holds a truly international throne,
Liverpool has art that is difficult to surpass,
With international; sporting heroes of our own.
Liverpool Football Club is a dominant world force,
And the Beatles pop music too, will reign of course.

Liverpool in Canada has as River Mersey though,
It's population is only 0.6% per cent of our own,
But East Liverpool Ohio is a city, larger and so,
And it's population has to eleven thousand has grown.
The Pier Head, Albert Dock and William Brown Street,
Are treasures a World Heritage Site status needs to meet!

Scandinavian Cruise

When we were boarding we were told to beware,
So my wife and I both carefully left the quay,
And walked up the gangway with particular care,
We boarded but our luggage was put on separately.
We were given the key to our cabin on board the ship,
And shown this luxury cabin that was ours for this trip.

We looked out across the clear blue, rippling sea,
As our cruise ship left dock and steamed ahead,
Soon the blue choppy waves were like a fantasy,
Because now we must, unpack and dress instead.
We sat with the captain at the captain's table to dine,
And we had a four course meal with vintage wine.

It is a very luxurious suite but our first cruise,
The dress code was evening suit and lady's gown,
So for dinner, anything less and they can refuse,
And for wearing a smart suit, people will certainly frown.
However with a smart selection of evening dress,
We dressed formally and we were bound to impress.

After having breakfast early we both played tennis,
And I quickly found that I am not at all fit,
Perhaps for eating out so much is this my Nemesis?
And before not very long I just had to sit.
After I had had my steam sauna I really did feel,
That the warm waters of our Jacuzzi would appeal.

The next day my wife and I had a relaxing swim,
We wanted to try to keep fit and show some drive,
So we exercised lightly to keep us quite in trim,
But neither of us were up to trying to dive.
I sat in the sun and breathed the Scandinavian air,
Viewing the bright blue sky; from a low soft chair.

Fjords from the Sky

We disembarked at Bergen to take in the view,
Looking down over the Fjords to the sea,
This trip we considered something we must do,
And flying over we thought of as a necessity.
The aeroplane makes four flights each day,
But it is a small plane so we decided to prepay.

The Fjords are deep and the water is dark blue,
The sky was bright and one can see for miles,
So with such majestic views we took photos too,
And we went out over the North Sea to see it's wiles.
The mistress of the sea shows her passion and fire,
Crashing against the rocks to, pronounce her desire.

From up in the sky we saw a school of whales,
Something we had not seen from the ship's deck,
And Norway is the place where the sun never pales,
But whales are shy, quiet and not easy to check.
Dolphin and whale hunting has a worldwide ban,
That is ignored mainly by Norway and Japan.

Our diverse exercise challenged us each day,
Rejuvenating our tired muscles with sport,
I must have lost some weight along the way,
But after my meal I drank brandy and port.
When our dinner has properly had time to digest,
We would proudly take the floor and dance our best.

With some other people we teamed up to have fun,
Some of whom had quite unusual things to do,
Like playing in a quiz whilst laying in the sun,
And judging a bikini beauty contest I did that too.
The ten days on board all too quickly passed,
But our cherished memories will forever last.

Lark

I am a bird, the Lark and I am wild and free,
Each and every day I am awake before the dawn,
Trying to awaken the world so that it can see,
What a beautiful new day the rising sun has born.
I would be just another small bird on the wing,
Until you see me fly and hear me so opulently sing.

All our species are passerine type birds,
I am six inches long and a small bird really,
I study the human and the human's words,
As they study me and my family sincerely.
Man knows that I am a musical and literary giant,
Like John Lennon I remain aloof and defiant.

This natural world is full of treasure and joy,
So it is on the ground that I will make my nest,
Because I am wild even though I am still coy,
But I can romantically sing to my mate and jest.
Spotting worms and insects from way up high,
I do to feed on, by diving out of the clear blue sky.

My partner and I are serious about breeding,
In fact only this month three eggs she has laid,
Soon I will start my job of continuously feeding,
Insects for our chicks so that they are well made.
Some parents serve seed, a low quality diet,
This is laziness to keep their own life so quiet.

I have a cream crest but dull, dark brown feathers,
This combination will camouflage me well,
My tough plumage keeps me dry in all weathers,
As I, would get drenched if the morning rain fell.
I explode with an enthusiastic operatic burst,
Which announces to all that I am well-versed.

Larks' Tune and Territory

I am only very small but I can drop like a stone,
To pick up unsuspecting insects to eat off the ground,
Then I will start singing and flying all alone,
And hope my mate hears this uniquely romantic sound.
I have hidden from many vicious birds of prey,
So my tonsils stay still when they come my way.

GM crops slowly poison the land where we live,
And huge man-made machines destroy our nests,
It is only man, the predator I will never forgive,
So I badly want to convert or terminate the pests.
In the country where GM farmers do persist,
Cross-pollination and poison will still exist.

All wild animal families are difficult to feed,
I work very hard so that my family and I can eat,
As all my hungry chicks want better than seed,
But this is an obligation that a father must meet.
After being out flying all day now I will walk,
Back, to my cosy nest again to sleep and talk.

I will keep our breeding territories away from harm,
Provide insects primarily for our chicks to eat,
The nutrient from live food has an energetic charm,
So our chicks have thick grey hair and are upbeat.
When chicks are young they should avoid seed,
For their long feathers they will need!

Our fluffy chicks we quickly have to wean,
Off the hazardous GM seed and on to live food,
Insects are safer to eat as no poison is seen,
And they eat insects without them being chewed.
I will have to show them what is caught,
Where, how and what should not be sought.

Power Sources

Most of our electricity is coal from a deep mine,
They are dirty, dusty and many are diseased,
But the end product is always clean and fine,
So the consumer has a right to be pleased.
Electricity travels to us at the speed of light,
So there is no waiting as it is a sheer delight.

The dirty fossil fuels such as coal and coke,
Are still our greatest; source of electrical power,
And burning them causes such dirty smelly smoke,
So that the air around us; is always misty and sour.
There are not plentiful resources of fossil fuels,
But the others are in such a minority, coal still rules.

From all of ninety-three million miles away,
The sun sends us bright solar power from afar,
It heats and lights our planet during the day,
So it can heat our homes or run a small car.
When the sun is very hot and really bright,
Then energy can be stored and generated at night.

Great Britain does not have a lot of very hot sun,
And our weather does not go to great extremes,
So solar-powered utilities and a laser gun,
Are figments of imagination and only in our dreams.
We could harness more energy to generate,
If more sun from solar power we could consolidate.

Hydraulic power comes from high water pressure,
Such as damming fast rivers or parts of lakes,
However the air is clean and it is much fresher,
So much electricity for us, our water makes.
If the sun shines constantly and all rain stops,
Some water will evaporate and the pressure drops.

Harnessing Power

If there is not enough real sunshine in the sky,
Then on solar power you can really not be sure,
But if there is a vast surplus of heat from on high,
Then water levels you can bet will be very poor.
This will definitely cause a shortage of water,
And hydraulic power it will also try to slaughter.

Alternative electricity is daylight solar power,
From a south facing house with panels on their roofs,
With panels on your roof you can have a shower,
This would make you think you are aloof.
The financial return which is tax free,
Depends on how much daylight your panels see.

Wind power produces a clean natural energy pill,
That is providing the windmills or sails blow,
If they are in the doldrums they will stand still,
As they rely upon the wind to gyrate and go.
Again it is from a clean natural source,
But the wind can often be deflated of course.

Power can be harnessed too from tidal waves,
And besides our island we have quite high tides,
Why not use their strength and make them our slaves,
Because the, rise and fall of the sea never subsides.
There could be hazards if ships were not aware,
Of where they, are and what they are doing there.

If it is at all possible to multiply the sun's rays,
Without the sun throwing out such extreme heat,
So that there are plenty of natural waterways,
Because technology like this would, be a treat.
Together the wind, sun and water are the solution,
To this, dirty energy with disease and pollution.

Wanted Dead

I live a scary and often quite a savage life,
But my family and I have to be provided for,
And it is clear man's feelings for me are quite rife,
That they don't want me or my kind anymore.
Humans have industrious lives and live on a farm,
So why do they want to hunt us and do us such harm?

For the odd fowl I am "Wanted Dead or Alive",
I am fearful of vicious hounds, who hunt in packs,
I could leave my family and hope they will survive,
If the, hunt would just be content to follow my tracks.
There are redcoats on horseback chasing after me,
And they blow loud horns in our serene country.

The redcoats have guard dogs on each farm,
They too do their master's dirty work, I fear,
And they frighten their visitors and often cause harm,
The public right of way though looks entirely clear.
There are hidden dogs in this foreboding atmosphere,
That will frighten tourists from walking around here.

Discriminating between the tourist and the fox,
The tourist can, armed with the law sue using the writ,
Whereas after stealing the odd hen from a wire box,
I can feed my family but the farmers have a fit!
I have an increasing number of sleepless nights,
Because no law at all protects an animal's rights.

The Rural Community is now in more danger,
Because it does not provide for what my family need,
With redcoats, packs of hounds and the forest ranger,
We run like the wind, die or just lie down and bleed.
When I was a cub we lived sedately and we had time to play,
Also we learned to kill, to feed ourselves the natural way.

Red Fox on the move

My vixen, our four cubs and I will leave,
The city may be worse so we may want to return,
But the sound of hunting hounds we will not grieve,
And at present our journey is our only concern.
Leaving the home you love will always be a pity,
But we believe that the climate is safer in the city.

When we arrived in town I went out for a meal,
And we came into some really good luck,
There was sat on a bin just ready for us to steal,
A whole, juicy, tasty Cantonese duck.
After all of us had rejoiced and been well-fed,
We wandered around the streets to find ourselves a bed.

There was an ideal hole for us to build our den,
Past a lake of sand, amongst some long grass and trees,
Eventually it was secure and big enough for ten,
By digging, adjoining holes under roots with ease.
Ours is an underground labyrinth sheltered by a tree,
We may not be so wild but from hounds we are free.

The Urban foxes all sleep and eat extremely well,
In fact Chinese food is an acquired taste,
And all the four cubs like it too I can tell,
Because nothing in our, lair ever goes to waste.
Sometimes we meet other foxes in the park,
And with our bright eyes go shopping in the dark.

On these gorgeous Chinese takeaway meals,
My four dear cubs are all now getting quite fat,
Food they can freely steal and I know how it feels,
But what could, I possibly do to remedy or curtail that?
Our home is clean very pleasant, warm and dry,
With no hounds, redcoats and food is in plentiful supply.

The Red Foxes' Future

I said if you eat too much and do too little exercise,
That you four cubs will struggle to get a mate,
As you are not sporty or handsome like the other guys,
And that you will never be until you lose some weight.
They all took my advice and soon two cubs had mates,
Proving that love swings through these romantic gates.

Now all of our four cubs are nearly fully grown,
Our eldest vixen, too, is fervently looking for a mate,
Her two older brothers are looking for places of their own,
And their vixens will have cubs after a three month wait.
I worry about my youngest; she is so naïve and shy,
And the sophisticated dogs all seem to pass on by.

The day Grandparents of mixed cubs will soon dawn,
Our eldest vixen and her older two brothers have all mated,
Three families and another generation will be born,
So bundles of fur and time for play will be created.
I worry about our youngest who is a shy vixen in her prime,
Who goes wandering in the countryside much of the time.

A wounded young dog fox was just left to bleed,
As his family were fleeing buckshot and the hunt,
Leaving him when they heard him cry, as if to plead,
They scurried away quickly hoping to sacrifice the runt.
The hounds missed the injured fox as he fell down the hill,
But now he was stuck, in great pain and had to be still.

He snapped at our youngest as it was a bit of a shock,
She pushed him into the water where he was now free,
Then she washed and licked his tormented hock,
To try to relieve the pain that he suffers from his injury.
With a log they floated and hopped down the stream,
My youngest and this crippled dog make a good team.

A Safe Haven

Two days and nights went by before they reached town,
But when they did there was Chinese food to eat,
As he was injured and without a family of his own,
He stayed and our youngest fussed upon him a treat.
Three months later three furry cubs were born,
So our youngest is a mother and no longer forlorn.

This is another notch carved on our family tree,
Because these fine cubs were purely a rural bred,
Not mixed like their cousins have turned out to be,
But like their Mum and Dad a fine rusty red.
We have many friends over three generations,
Now a better quality of life than was our expectations.

My vixen and I regularly visit friends and the in-laws,
To see how they are and who is having cubs yet,
And when we can hope to hear the patter of tiny paws,
We know that someone's dreams have now been met.
To think I was once hungry and a wild rural fox,
I am now secure but I have a rusty coat and black socks.

We have a great community growing up here,
Of mixed foxes of totally grey foxes and the rusty red,
We don't have vicious humans on horseback to fear,
And no ferocious dogs to maul you until you are dead.
The chef from the Chinese restaurant often chases us,
But he is slow, not vicious and he just makes a fuss.

We help with the Urban Fox Community Association,
So it is open for sport, leisure and culture in the park,
For every single urban fox of any generation,
In the summer in the barn and in the winter after dark!
This community has food and shelter that makes it secure,
No dog, his vixen and his cubs could ask for more.

Four Car Family

There are four motor car drivers in our home,
Now that Ian has finally passed his driving test,
My family, like gypsies are meant to roam,
So now the kids will not be such a pest.
Ian was firmly told not to drive his Mum's Saab,
Because; of the high performance of this twin-carb.

I first learnt to drive over twenty years ago,
When there were very few cars on the road,
And each vehicle there was, was relatively slow,
So driving then was in a much safer mode.
At that time there really was no motorcar finer,
Than; our reliable and treasured Morris Minor.

Great demands and advanced technology means,
Bigger and safer cars with a smoother ride,
All much faster and more powerful machines,
With power-assisted steering to stop you turning wide.
If you keep up with all the advances in driving,
Then you will not be the one who is left striving.

My wife used to drive competitively in car rallies,
So Jill, my lovely wife is particularly skilled,
And Ian thinks that his driving skill also tallies,
Because he is confident, young and strong willed.
Jill's car and Ian so often disappear,
But my wife's reprimands are extremely austere!

Jane, Ian's sister tends to exercise due care,
She does not drive her car excessively fast,
She reads the road signs so she is well aware,
Of the dangers of speed that are not forecast.
Jill thinks it is time now that Jane really feels,
Advanced, driving manoeuvres on her wheels.

Verve and Drive

Ian at present has a great macho teenage fad,
For fast girls, fast cars and fast food,
He has also said that he wants his own pad,
But who will look after this prestigious dude.
He will be the victim of fair weather friends,
Who will only stay with him until his luck ends.

Jill and I decided really for his, own sake,
That Ian should have a motor car a mini perhaps,
A car that is fairly slow and has a good brake,
So that he should not fall into speed traps.
Jill and I have paid many speeding fines before,
So he will not have many points left anymore.

If he has three more points put on his licence,
He will have twelve points and a long ban,
Accept for an appeal on the said offence,
He could not work then driving their van.
Ian would soon realise that with disqualification,
Soon follows a period of immobilization.

Jane works in a bank where luxury has brought her,
It is a Japanese hybrid, a Lexus GS to please,
With V6 engine and powerful electric motor,
Smooth to ride and space for one's knees.
This luxury shows her clients she has good taste,
And it can reach 60 in six seconds, if she raced.

Ian must now learn to earn his Mother's trust;
Only then will she give him a driving education,
Take him for a spin and kick up some dust,
And give him a taste of this addictive sensation.
Jill will not let Ian drive that Saab of hers,
Unless he improves a lot, to earn his spurs!

Koppites

The Liverpool F. C. reds have the Anfield tune,
Sung by their supporters to make the Mersey sound,
After the whistle blows on a Saturday afternoon,
Their music is magic and will lift the football ground.
The Liverpool Football Club will Never Walk Alone,
Because its great football team is so well known.

We have more trophies than any other team,
Our supporters sing along with passion and skill,
Whereas other clubs can only wish or dream,
That, their players were urged with, such vocal will.
More than forty thousand people sing as one,
And wave scarves until the final whistle has gone.

All fans pay homage to the famous Spion Kop,
Which was built; at Anfield Liverpool in 1906,
It is high and daunting like a hill at the very top,
And was built after; Everton had picked up sticks.
The battle of Spionkop was against the Boers,
To; occupy South Africa and stop their wars.

The mast that the British soldiers had brought,
Still stands tall in the Kop at Anfield,
To commemorate all the men who had fought,
And to show everyone that we will never yield.
We won the battle of Spion Kop but not the war,
So then farmers ruled South Africa once more.

Until the Hillsborough disaster, that came in 1989,
Our players had the confidence and determination,
That made Liverpool's dominance there divine,
But since then we only win the odd consolation.
The Liverpool fans had an MP that they would call,
But she was just too lazy to be bothered at all.

Crooked Police, Press and Government

Into police computers the press do not hack,
They just ask a "Peeler" and for a monkey or two,
To get an informer as "Bobby" won't get the sack,
In fact a promotion looms for more than just a few.
On the first inquest a bent coroner saw it derailed,
Dishonest police and a criminal press prevailed.

The Policemen should save life and not blame,
But on that day they stood and just watched,
Or telephoned the press about a drunken game,
So the cruel policemen meant the rescue was botched.
Not letting the ambulances in meant lives were lost,
And this disaster meant we are still counting the cost.

Until a genuine independent enquiry is conducted,
And establishes that the media and the police lied,
New mental foundations can not be constructed,
Until justice prevails, for all those who died!
The police closed ranks and prosecution they elude,
West Midlands Police had Yorkshire Police collude.

When Thatcher's Irish gang culture had gone,
We are still waiting for the IRA to abate,
Justice from phone hacking we still have none,
And no policemen have suffered a true fate.
There are ninety seven Liverpool fans not alive,
After twenty five years will justice <u>ever</u> survive?

The press often illegally gains information,
Mostly they hack a person's mobile telephone,
Other times they will hack e-mails for a sensation,
They will also bribe the police it is known.
Then there is a conundrum for us of course,
Is there any honesty left in today's police force?

American Wilderness

Grizzly Bears are scavengers and they eat fruit,
But they are really an omnivore and will steal food,
Dead farm animals and picnic baskets all will suit,
 To, give it the fat to keep it in a good mood.
A Bear could kill even a Moose if it could get near,
 But Bears are too slow and lazy to catch Deer.

Cougars can stalk various animals for many a mile,
 But they have an area of many females to attend,
As they reproduce in large numbers all the while,
 And for their numerous families they need to fend.
Mountain Lions and Coyotes have the stealth to wait,
 And feeding too soon will seal the Coyote's fate.

A Cougar will often go into rural areas like a farm,
 For a sheep, a calf or any sizeable piece of meat,
To feed his many families just where is the harm,
Foxes, wild birds and rodents will feed on his retreat.
Man assumes ownership of cattle, horses and sheep,
 Even though they are not primates or man's to keep.

Coyotes wait to scavenge a piece of dead meat,
 Condors can steal from the sky during the day,
That is after the carnivore has had enough to eat,
 All scavengers feed on dripping meat this way.
In fear of theft or in case its killer should return,
They eat their food quickly with a guilty concern.

Birds of prey feed from pieces of live meat,
 The animal can be either predator or prey,
But an injured animal will never admit defeat,
 If fact it will fight tooth and nail all the way.
Vultures have weak talons but a very strong beak,
Quite; strong enough to tear off a meaty streak.

Hunters and Their Prey

The Falcon, Eagle, Osprey, Hawk and Owl,
All can fly many hundreds of miles,
And they can pluck rats, mice and even a foul,
Up, from the ground with their individual styles.
They can dive from a thousand feet in the sky,
To catch, a mouse on the ground, just scurrying by.

The Elk, the Moose, the Caribou and the Deer,
Are mammals that are North American herbivores,
And can be food if their predators get too near,
But usually they can escape their predators' jaws.
They have long strong legs and can move very fast,
And their pursuers' speed just does not last.

Antlers are grown by both male and female Caribou,
But it is just the male with all other kinds of Deer,
However if a Cougar or a Mountain Lion came too,
Then the Deer and their antlers will run to disappear.
Big predatory cats have the energy to track all day,
And usually they slay an injured or young as prey.

These handsome four legged animals are fair game,
But the Moose they will leave to Men and Bears,
Because they are much bigger and not so tame,
Besides they kill for food not for sport or wares.
If a predator were to trap a Moose and be near,
The Moose might kick and kill out of panic or fear.

Over all the vast animal kingdom man does rein,
So man should surely have a handicap of a sort,
Simply because of the superior size of his brain,
Imagine killing with a rifle just for the sport.
When man kills an animal, is it relatively clean?
Less pain will be felt and fewer open wounds are seen?

Heavenly Earth

I am a land composite and I am the soil,
I have many variables like sand, peat and clay,
People with spades work very hard and toil,
Just to dig up grass and potatoes each day.
Why do you dig up potatoes to eat?
They have carbohydrates and they are no real treat.

First and foremost I must robustly complain,
About the number of illegal migrants called weeds,
If I had my way they would all be slain,
But man keeps them often for decorative needs.
This is not how man should treat his best friend,
Mother Earth who will stay with him until the end!

In a totally different environment of my land,
There are friendly carrots that are firmly knit,
And for them there must be plenty of fine sand,
So that the water can, seep right through it.
Carrots must always be sown firm and deep,
So as to straighten them when, you come to reap.

Carrots will grow in a sandy soil with ease,
When eaten they can help you see in the dark,
And eating them will help fight many a disease,
You can also control your weight without being a nark.
They are about six inches from top to tape,
And are bright red in colour and of a conical shape.

Both shaped like balls are turnips and swedes,
Their flesh is very hard, juicy and yellow,
Although they will meet all of your needs,
Because after cooking, they will soften and mellow.
After you have peeled or cut off their dirty skin,
You can put it out for refuse in the dustbin.

Open Accommodation

Cabbages and carrots are planted in burrows,
They are spaced about a foot apart to grow in a line,
To thrive on the sheer richness of my furrows,
And to produce prize vegetables on which you can dine.
These tasty vegetables do provide you with stealth,
And you eat plenty of them to better your health.

Some plants are not just extremely hungry,
Cabbages and potatoes both show their greed,
Often they leave me practically nutrient free,
So that next year recuperation is what I need.
After those two vegetables have been I fear,
I will need to rest for the following year.

This is called by farmers "Crop Rotation",
If I am not rested my quality will decrease,
So for good quality and good motivation,
For a year my industrial growth will cease.
I will be fed and nurtured for a year of ease,
And start off slowly on sprouts and peas.

Perennial plants which are difficult to uproot,
Are what grows all around my gorgeous field,
They have thick deep rooted hedges that bear fruit,
Usually blackberries are the fruit that they yield.
Come summer their fruit is ripe and picked by hand,
And people herd on me and trample on my land.

Fruit trees can have asexual or sexual reproduction,
Propagation is natural and will have both genes,
This sexual act can happen for tree reconstruction,
And genes of both parents are done by this means.
Asexual is done by grafting, rootstock like cloning,
And have us soil twisting, turning and moaning.

Australian Resources

The original Aborigine people were there first,
A proud native race that does not understand,
Why they have been ignored, robbed and cursed,
Primarily by, English criminals to steal their land.
The native Aborigines still parade themselves bare,
Without proper shelter, a Spartan life they wear.

One marsupial that Australia has is a Kangaroo,
They have two limbs free and they kind of crouch,
Kangaroos also have a pouch on their stomach too,
So they can shield their infants in this fleshy pouch.
The Kangaroo is on Australia's fine coat of arms,
Business, sport and currencies all use its charms.

Australia has another marsupial the Koala bear,
That lives and eats in Eucalyptus trees without fear,
This nocturnal, big eyed herbivore is very rare,
And Koalas have their marsupial pouch at the rear.
We warm to these lovely, furry, toy-like creatures,
As soft and loveable are some of their features.

The Great Barrier Reef is off Queensland's coast,
It is in water, less than five hundred feet deep,
The reef grows where the sun shines the most,
With nearly three thousand individual reefs to keep!
The Great Barrier Reef can be seen from outer space,
Like the Great Wall of China it has a universal grace.

The Great Barrier Reef is very much alive,
With orgasms, reefs, fishes, plant, and algae,
So many different life forms all survive,
Here in the tropical waters of the Coral Sea.
For over half a million years the reef has been growing,
With the sun's rays into the shallow waters glowing.

 # *Politics and way of Life*

In nineteen hundred and one came independence,
But Australia kept the pound sterling until 1910,
Then the Australian Dollar replaces pounds and pence,
This was easier because Britain wasn't digital then.
The Australian Dollar is a currency in the top eight,
It comes much higher than China's Yaun which is great.

With independence a democratic country it became,
Soon many big businesses came to make money,
There were politicians but no one really to blame,
And now many beautiful horizons are not so sunny.
Richie Benaud is a straight talking guy an Aussie guy,
Their cricket captain and Channel Four broadcaster is why!

For export the Australians make quite good wines,
It is quality white wine unlike the American junk,
Another business that thrives are their diamond mines,
Most of which come from shafts De Beers have sunk.
In a tin there is also Four X, the real Aussie Beer,
That is brewed in dear old England, right here.

Australia is vast; tinder dry and very little grows,
The sheep pull the grass right out from the root,
They sheer sheep for their wool and export clothes,
As a sheep's fleece is a warm and a woolly fruit.
Sheep are slaughtered for mutton and lamb as meat,
Tasty and lean so often exported for others to eat.

Sydney is the capital and a modern city, yet unique,
Now with cultures that all of the world shares,
The famous Sydney Harbour Bridge we will seek,
And of course the Sydney Opera House of theirs.
Some people sit in Brisbane with passion together,
All at the Gabba listening for willow on leather.

Concorde Experience

If you fly Concorde you really travel in style,
One of one hundred passengers and eight crew,
Flying faster than a bullet or a Cruise missile,
Crossing the Atlantic; at a speed of Mach 2.
With brilliant engines made by Rolls Royce,
And 25 years of passenger service to rejoice.

The world's most beautiful and talked about nose,
Leads Concorde distinctly through the skies,
And is not on a face set in a permanent pose,
Placed between, someone's red lips and blue eyes.
Concorde is a handsome and luxurious aircraft,
Certainly the most beautiful machine ever draft.

No other aircraft has been tested in such detail,
Now vast safety improvements have been made,
So the continued success of Concorde can prevail,
To, safely lead the way in the air transport trade.
The safest way to travel is to fly on Concorde,
Because the years have shown it has an excellent record.

From the legendary flagship of the BA fleet,
Comes a 5 star service in the lounge and on board,
And any needs you have they will always meet,
As it, is good to know that your comfort is assured.
Your comfort and rest will come to no harm,
Because flying so fast has such a relaxing calm.

You will eat quality food that is a culinary delight,
Each is a "designer meal", tailored to suit your palate,
Five courses will be served by the staff in flight,
With: beverages, champagne, chardonnay and claret.
Then a glass of port or brandy you may just feel,
Would help you to digest such a satisfying meal.

Concorde is Quality

The BA staff are always impeccably dressed,
Giving far better service than any 5 star hotel,
Swiftly and efficiently your needs are addressed,
And politely with care they boast a smile as well.
Helpful co-operation means that right from the start,
Your host cares for you right from the heart.

It cruises at a height of about 58 thousand feet,
From London to New York which is 3,670 miles,
In less than three hours it is a record few fighters can beat,
And it undermines competitors who it really riles.
Concorde can cross the Atlantic twice in one day,
Between London, Heathrow and New York, JFK.

A legend in its own lifetime, fly the flag, fly BA,
Because this voyage is a journey of yours to relish,
With excitement and opulence there on display,
And as long as you live this memory you will cherish.
It is like a time machine, or vehicle of fiction,
As travelling First Class could become an addiction!

The patriotic French and British want Concorde to fly,
Not sold as museum pieces or worse given to the Yanks,
Set it up as a Business Class Airline and then see why,
With, room in future for plenty of profit and thanks.
We could demutualise Concorde and make it a plc,
And sell its shares to the public on the CAC and the FTSE.

Sadly the French and British governments had lost out,
But being taken out of service was still a surprise,
Boundaries of aircraft technology had been crossed,
And orders for new fighters and airliners arise.
A sad day particularly for the business class,
Because they are regular users and they have the brass.

Barn Owl Territory

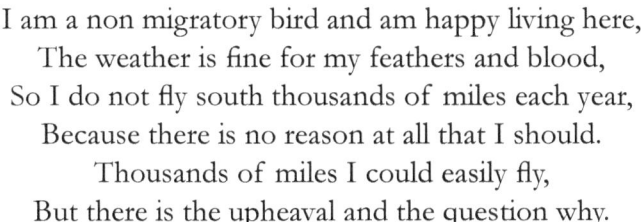

I am the Barn Owl and I am a big nocturnal bird,
I sit on the barn roof or on the branch of a tree,
Watching carefully but saying not a single word,
Just waiting in, the night for a, meal to come to me.
I sleep all day and come out for the night skies,
And I sit patiently in silence, waiting to surprise.

I am a non migratory bird and am happy living here,
The weather is fine for my feathers and blood,
So I do not fly south thousands of miles each year,
Because there is no reason at all that I should.
Thousands of miles I could easily fly,
But there is the upheaval and the question why.

I perch uncomfortably on rocks and hilltops too,
Waiting for something to rustle in the leaves below,
When it does, then I feel that a tasty meal is due,
And silently my wings open and I swiftly flow.
With my large sharp talons I can easily snatch,
Most small vermin like mice; they're a tasty catch.

My favourite food is tender young vole,
This is a speciality enticement that an owl picks,
And I often catch them staggering from their hole,
But voles are smart and often win with rodent tricks.
I eat like a medieval king as cutlery I do not need,
My talons will tear meat, for my wide beak to feed.

Any dirty barn, nook or cranny can be our home,
Most furnishings we use are only wood or hay,
So in the woods and dry fields I will usually comb,
For bits, to make a nest where my chicks and I can stay.
Humans think that we wise birds are no real match,
But if challenged we will bite and fiercely scratch.

Barn Owl Bird of Prey

All owls are efficient and extremely wise,
Our wings are multi-feathered, large and light,
We each have big appetites and big, deep, dark eyes,
And we can see for miles around in the dead of night.
I use little energy as my wings let me float on air,
And I look well built because exercise is rare.

I am a pedigree bird you can tell by my tail,
Because in flight it has a flickering motion,
My wings are soft, light, large and never fail,
They carry me many miles over the land and the ocean.
I am between nine and eighteen inches long,
A pale brown all over and my wings are very strong.

Coming in over bogs, woodlands, farmlands or dirt,
There are about thirty sub-species of my kind of bird,
All over the world except in the polar region and desert,
We are the experts who fly in low and escape unheard.
We are called names like Silver, White, and Rat,
Also Death, Straw, Stone and Cave like my habitat.

It is now time that their genes were passed on,
So in Spring as many as a dozen eggs are laid,
But courtship varies and some couples have none,
As birds are fierce and their status is on parade.
I am a male owl so I do many courtship flights,
Some end up with competitors wanting fights.

If my dear Missus is worried or hunting on her own,
Then she or I will hoot loudly in the cool night air,
Because this is what you do without a mobile phone,
As clearly it is essential that I communicate with her.
My hoot is an eerie sound of "to whit to woo",
And that unique call is the only one owls do.

The Wheel

Ever since the invention of the wheel,
Man has profited from this machine's power,
Movement now has a greater and more advanced appeal,
Since cart-horses struggled with this blooming flower.
Horses will struggle much less with their load,
If they are not, dragging it along an uneven road.

Soon vehicles with wheels came to roll along,
And dragging along was not the fashion any more,
For sheer efficiency a wheel can not be wrong,
So wheelwrights and grooms now came to the fore.
More cargo could be pulled on these large carts,
To access new business in much further, parts.

First came a metal frame that was built for one,
With a cog and chain for man to sit and ride,
But that was a vehicle that would never catch on,
Because gentleman; always like to sit aloof in pride.
When the bicycle or penny farthing was born,
Gentlemen had them and their trousers got worn.

In later years rich people would have a motor car,
The lower-class and women would each have a bike,
Factory workers and ladies used to ride them far,
As it, brings exercise and economical travel alike.
Then the shape was changed and not just a few,
A massive cycle industry then started to brew.

Riches in cargo needed to move at a fantastic pace,
With manure from the horses and with no pollution,
But in England now it became a competitive race,
With the first train and the industrial revolution!
For horses it was starting to be the end of the line,
As another form of power for a while will be fine.

Fuels for Power

Steam engine trains were fuelled by coal,
A powerful industrial machine of course,
With engines that forced the wheels to roll,
And they became known as man's iron horse.
Such powerful locomotives emit much smoke,
Easily enough emissions for any, man to choke.

With such dirty emissions we are nearly up to date,
With the smoky internal combustion engine here,
And the power that is needed to move more freight,
But the air is intensely dirty and very far from clear.
If we used energy that did not pollute like fire,
It would be clean, natural and will not expire.

Clean energy was rarely used because it was weak,
To replace the steam engine did not work well,
Cleaning up the skies seems like a losing streak,
But power rules and sluggish engines don't sell.
However the diesel engine arrived on the scene,
That is dirty and noisy but is a more powerful machine.

Some hypoid cars are in the market-place,
Cleaner than petrol or diesel but they are not cheap,
Tax advantages for such vehicles is commonplace,
But in time if there is something better they will keep.
Comfort is now more important than high speed,
And safety and control are both paramount indeed.

The wind, the sun and water all come free,
They are natural resources we should now heed,
To provide us efficiently with clean electricity,
To, power our vehicles to an ample safe speed.
With power used like wind, water and light;
The earth will be cleaner because transport is in sight.

Our Daily H₂O

The rain falls down from dark clouds in the sky,
Grey Cumulo-Nimbus is an aerial filling station,
It pours water into our rivers and lakes close by,
And the power it creates is quite a sensation.
As long as we have grey clouds we will know,
That our, fresh water will continue to flow.

Hard water all has mineral contents present,
Whilst it does not pose a hazard to your health,
It brings limescale deposits that are unpleasant,
And replacing your boiler is bad for you wealth.
The likes of dish washers and boilers are unclean,
And one will soon have to replace the machine.

Hospitals sterilise their equipment it is their rules,
To keep surgeries free from dirt and disease,
So they heat water to keep sterile the hospital's tools,
Because bacteria can come from just a sneeze!
Death can follow when bacteria and disease are rife,
But sterilisation can mean a prolonged life.

Depending on over what kind of land it has run,
Will determine whether your water is soft or hard,
Cleansing and adding fluoride will need to be done,
But the earth beneath it will be permanently scarred.
Water is a liquid hydrogen and oxygen compound,
But often traces of acids and limestone are found.

Water companies try to get rid of the waste,
They treat it with chemicals in case it is diseased,
And dispose of it safely with great haste,
So that people are safe and the environment is pleased.
We have clean water to cook, wash and drink,
Without this, disease would spread rampantly I think.

Water is Life

Water for all is the sign that life can be born,
Not just on Earth but on other planets too,
Because when water comes, then life will dawn,
But not necessarily as plants and animals do.
Life can be insects, plankton, soil or shells,
Be invisible, be static and have reproductive cells.

Some planets can be seen with life and light,
Sometimes many millions of light years from Earth,
Out in a jungle of lonely, desert and night,
With jewels of wisdom; what are they worth.
Some planets must have life in each constellation,
And humans may even be a distant relation.

Musical bells of water chime the font of true life,
It is delivered to us through pipes each day,
But sometimes it causes much trouble and strife,
If it is poisoned or does not come our way.
Too much of a good thing is a very true verse,
Because when your house is flooded, it is a real curse.

Our unpredictable climate explodes with tears,
It can flood the roads with a prolonged heavy burst,
Rivers and lakes overflow badly some years,
Leaving dirty water that won't quench your thirst.
A flooded home will cause much damage and despair,
But Mother Nature says she just does not care.

Conversely if the sun is hot and there is no rain,
Fresh tap water can become very scarce,
As each of our reservoirs will tend to drain,
And unless it rains, the situation will get worse.
In panic people will fill all their pots and pans,
In case legal restrictions spoil their plans.

The Importance of Water

Such drastic measures can sometimes mean,
The frugal use of showers and hosepipe bans,
Often staying dirty instead of washing clean,
Consequently the water companies have no fans.
The plants in a dry garden have to suffer in pain,
While hosepipes are banned and there is no rain.

Seldom does anybody in England die of thirst,
Even if the land is barren and reservoirs are dry,
We only need to wish that a large cloud would burst,
To drop, torrents of water, down from the sky.
By conserving usage and all pulling together,
We are always prepared for prolonged hot dry weather.

When water is plentiful and there is no dry spell,
No, floodwater nor stormy rains in excess,
With no broken pipes the water is flowing quite well,
But people do not recognise this industrious success.
England has no monsoons but time and time again,
When unscheduled showers come, we will complain.

Sometimes the rain will spoil our national game,
So we have tea until the pitch sufficiently dries,
But the wicket is soft instead of being the same,
And after rain disturbs cricket it is the bowler's prize.
When the sun shines down on a drying pitch,
It turns sticky and the pickings for spinners are rich.

Rain, like a woman will come but is often late,
For she tops up our rivers, reservoirs and lakes,
And rescues our land from a dry miserable state,
With the, richly treasured moisture that she makes.
In equatorial countries people frequently die of thirst,
In sandy deserts or the ocean; which of them is worst?

Troutbeck

I am the wily but native Rainbow Trout,
I am the smartest of all the fresh water fishes,
But there are natural enemies and fishermen about,
Who would kill me and eat me against my wishes.
Fishermen will stand in a busy wide river and wait,
Hoping that, I will come along to take their bait.

Fishermen have an egotistical unsporting attitude,
Fancy having to try to catch us while we feed,
It is just like putting VAT on our food,
They are taxing necessities out of pure greed.
If we, the Trout are caught we are really no feast,
And the only religion we get is from their priest.

Does my colour or speed sting a fisherman's eyes?
Does my uncanny cunning drive them insane?
Is it the challenge which I lay down what they despise?
Or is it the ease with which I escape time and time again?
Do my survival skills hurt a swollen human pride?
As they so often end up on the losing side.

We Rainbow Trout execute these jungle rules,
Often in places where fishermen fear to wade,
Mostly in the deep, dark rocky bedded pools,
Where my family live while my eggs are being laid.
If one were hungry and wants a real family meal,
Go somewhere that still has plenty to steal.

Proud fishermen still tell such rotten lies,
About that really big fish that only just got away,
When it was not so big it was only my size,
But that is not what a fisherman would say!
Nobody ever believes these fishermens' feats,
Particularly not when told, by such big cheats.

The Trout Community

The Trout, the River Fox has much influence,
Where the river is long and often quite steep,
From the river's source to the river's confluence,
When, sometimes the waters are fast and deep.
The fishermen though have some easy game,
With several populous fishes who are quite tame.

My influence really does not much extend,
To those two legged, long monsters in green,
Who come here brazenly with a rod and pretend,
That they; the fishermen belong on our scene.
We, the natural water residents here are bitter,
With humans, their tackle and their filthy litter!

We hate these two legged pompous strangers,
With a clumsy manner and macho egos to fulfil,
They bring us all sorts of unforeseen dangers,
Coming into our rivers with their licence to kill!
Hunting us with a thin luring line and pole,
Hoping they can trick us and claim our soul.

We the Trout refuse to bend or live in fear,
Green primates without their tails or hairy skins,
Are just humans in disguise who trespass here,
To kill, to hide or to shed their depressing sins!
A comprehensive range of river life does reside,
So do not expect us to swallow our pride!

Our crystal clear river in places swiftly flows,
And into our river comes tributaries and streams,
It is wild, natural and in deep forested throes,
To keep away the urban jungle like fishing teams.
Where we live we want clean air and tasty flies,
Running water and places with clear blue skies.

Family and Neighbours

I look for my lunch with astuteness and care,
My favourite diet is a damsel fly or a fire fly,
But if a fisherman's hook is hanging there,
Then authentic danger lurks so I will pass by.
I also particularly like for lunch pheasant's tail,
Or the Mayfly providing the sun doesn't fail.

We, the Trout are freshwater fish of course,
In neither the salt sea nor the stagnant lakes,
Trout are strong and can swim against the force,
As all Salmonidae fish have the power it takes.
In the coastal sea you will sometimes find,
A Sea Trout, a fish who has changed its mind!

I am neither a vicious monster nor a Bream,
But a very strong line you will need to cast,
More strength from my hunter I can easily redeem,
Because I am clever, camouflaged and fast.
I do not weigh much on the fisherman's scale,
But a broken line should tell quite a tale.

Trout generally are not as big as Roach,
But of fighting cunning I am blessed in the first degree,
As a prize stealth weapon I will often poach,
By sticking, lines and hooks firmly into a floating tree.
Only Rainbow Trout very green around the gills,
Would be caught by naive and obvious human skills!

Just what would these Green Monsters not give?
To stick their thieving feathered hooks in me,
I am determined to have a full rich long life to live,
And to swim freely for many years totally "scot" free.
I am not a vicious carnivore like a fearsome Pike,
And it is only noisy dirty fishermen I dislike!

Distant Trout Relatives

We Rainbow Trout are statuesque and we are not fond,
Particularly of a Goldfish paying for so much,
They are inferior and only belong in a small pond,
Or is it me that is old fashioned and out of touch?
I really do not want to drink, eat or harp,
With something that is really only a Carp.

Most Americans call us an aka Steelhead,
Our salt-water cousins live in the Pacific,
Others live in the Great Lakes it has been said,
So we are quite cosmopolitan and not specific.
I can swim all day and from dusk to dawn,
And at the age of four I will swim upstream to spawn.

The Scottish Salmon are really quite amorous,
But all too often they meet with their fate,
Undignified laying face down and unglamorous,
With potatoes and vegetables cooked on a plate.
They are sometimes preserved and put into a tin,
But either way the salmon dies and does not win.

Salmon are called the "River Mountaineers",
As when the time is ripe and their spawning calls,
They will conquer their quest and have no fears,
And will swim up fast flowing and steep waterfalls.
The Salmon is a large silvery relative of mine,
Who eat similar flies to me when they dine.

The Kingfisher's breast is a very bright red,
But it dives into the water very fast and steep,
With it's beak charging on whatever is ahead,
So an alert eye for Kingfishers we need to keep.
This is an airborne greedy fish-eating crook,
That has a charming and pretty innocent look.

Enemies at Large

Kingfishers are enemies and they are no fools,
They rely upon nutritious fish for their diet,
Which they will find in still, shallow pools,
In good light with no wind; where it is quiet.
Easier to catch are Chubb, Bream and Roach,
Carp are too small and Pike it wouldn't approach.

Other aerial enemies are many birds of prey,
Who fly gracefully with human-like spikes,
They come with a keen eye looking our way,
To dive from the sky for a fish that it likes.
These birds are nasty, ugly vicious creatures,
That snatch fish with their claw-like features.

From Hawks and Owls we have enough to fear,
Falcons fly and stun fish before making a lift,
Kestrels and Eagles skim the surface or very near,
Then grip tightly with barbed talons their tasty gift.
Predominantly the Osprey is in a class of its own,
And I am a jolly foxy character with backbone.

Pike are freshwater fish and a vicious predator,
And a fisherman hopefully could get a good bite,
From surely the river's worst fish carnivore,
Now that scrap would be a real good prize fight!
We being "Gaming Fish" have all placed our bets,
On either the Pike's teeth or the fisherman's nets!

When a Pike swims by, close in our river,
There is usually a riot to shelter in the clear,
Because the Pike is deadly and will deliver,
Quite quickly mass murder, chaos and abject fear!
It is at our family's peril us Game fish ignores,
Such large teeth and strong devastating jaws!

Troubeck's Vicious

The Otter is a mammal but still a river resident,
With big strong teeth and a large appetite,
And of all our enemies they have set a president,
They are unique as we have so little for a fight.
Otters have webbed feet and can swim very fast,
So we need to be extra vigilant until they are past.

Humans have mass hunted Otters too,
They live on the riverbank in their own Holt,
So that Otter numbers are at present relatively few,
And when men and dogs come, they have to bolt.
Men hunted them for the shiny oily fur off their back,
As sport, with dogs and guns, humans did attack.

The law stops all hunting of the otter and the fox,
But it has forgotten all of us in freshwater,
So we will have to guide man as if we are the "Cox",
Otherwise we await various kinds of man's slaughter.
The Rainbow Trout needs proper legislation,
To, protect it from unsociable propagation.

The law has not included the Trout to it's list,
Is this because they resent our presence here,
And humans think torture we can easily resist,
Well I can say we "Can Not" I hope that is clear!
Danger in the river comes from brambles and hooks,
Also predatory fish try to spoil my good looks.

The Rainbow Trout possess receptors of great pain,
Usually by, a physical wound, poisoned water or air,
Although my medical plight has been in vain,
But behavioural and physiological changes occur.
The Edinburgh Roslin Institute know how we react,
And the amount of pain we need or can suffer to survive.

Jivah Poetry Books

Ian Harris is the sole owner of all the Jivah Poetry Books which have small colour pictures or, cartoons to compliment them. These books are not ordinary hardback books they are Royal size (9.5"x 6.25"). They all have quality gloss paper inside the books and they each have a dust-jacket as a gloss cover on the outside. Much of this poetry tries to tell a story or give information.

The Jivah Poetry Book Collection will be:

1.   **Jivah World Poetry:**

This poetry book is educational and tries to quench the thirst that children have for knowledge and debate. It targets Animals, Geography, History and the Environment, and when some species have their quality of life improved by change other species are deprived. It is not always man so this is open for debate. While some of this book is fiction nearly all of it has a factual base.

2.   **Jivah Peoples Poetry**

This poetry book is nearly all fiction but it highlights the attitudes of snobbery and the differences that gender, ethnicity and education bring to everyday life. This is pronounced in employment, business and with the justice system. A white man that went to Oxford University would have no problem finding work, have a court find in his favour or be able to take out a loan if he so chooses.

3.   **Jivah Action Poetry:**

Jivah Action Poetry deals with sport, drama and some history. This is part fiction and part truth but always I will stress a point. This poetry will show you what part sport plays in our everyday lives and how it brings together people of all ethnicities, education and background there is still an ever widening gap with regards to gender. The England Ladies Cricket Team has done better than the men recently and so have England Ladies Football Team.

www.ingramcontent.com/pod-product-compliance
Lightning Source LLC
Chambersburg PA
CBHW070133100426
42744CB00009B/1823